EMERGING
SHAPES
of
the
Church

DAVID S. SCHULLER

The Witnessing Church Series

William J. Danker, Editor

Concordia Publishing House, St. Louis, Missouri
Concordia Publishing House Ltd., London, E. C. 1
© 1967 Concordia Publishing House
Library of Congress Catalog Card No. 67-12901
MANUFACTURED IN THE UNITED STATES OF AMERICA

Contents

v

Foreword

The law of life is: "Adapt or perish." The dinosaurs died out because the climate changed but they did not. Man is proving to be a remarkably adaptable creature. The human organism is even adjusting to the unearthly conditions of flight into space.

It takes a revolutionary church to survive and accomplish its task in a revolutionary world. The early apostles were identified as "they that have turned the world upside down."

There are Biblical limits beyond which we may not go in recasting changing forms, but it is fatally easy to identify our present vested interests, prejudices, and preferences with Biblical functions instead of allowing form to follow function. What are the limits of form? The Gospel must be rightly preached, the sacraments properly administered. Within these wide limits there is liberty. Within the broad confines of the Biblical functions of witness, worship, service, fellowship, and nurture, there is always room for stern self-criticism and appropriate change in form. Ongoing self-examination with concomitant change for the better is the church's counterpart of the individual's ongoing repentance. The Holy Spirit works through forms, but forms are not His master, rather His channels and His servants. John Ph. Koehler said, "The Gospel creates its own forms."

The life-giving Spirit operates through Christians whom He has endowed for His work. One of His gifted servants has described emerging shapes of the church in a series of lectures delivered to the 10th annual Institute on the Church in Mission, Aug. 30 to Sept. 3, 1965, at Concordia Seminary, St. Louis, Missouri. There was a very wide and general demand that they should be published.

The author, who earned a doctorate in sociology at St. Louis University, is remarkably well equipped to assess current trends and indicate possible future directions which emerging forms of the church may take in contemporary society.

At Concordia Seminary, students of pastoral theology, preaching, and the urban church had missed one of their favorite professors for a time while Dr. Schuller completed the unique experience that lies behind this book. These lectures come fresh from his service during the past 2 years as the Director of Urban Seminars, Division of Christian Life and Mission, National Council of the Churches of Christ in the U. S. A. This position was made possible by a Ford Foundation grant.

"The basic presupposition," Dr. Schuller explains, "was that most clergymen were faced with problems today for which their previous seminary training had not adequately equipped them. Most of these men did not adequately understand the structures and processes of modern urban life. The goal therefore was to establish a dialog between the academic community and the religious leadership of the given city. It was felt that the university has inside resources which the leadership of the churches needed. It was significant that the program was held at this time, for it is in these very years that universities are seeking their community, while the churches are beginning to ask about their role in the service of the whole man.

"A group of men representing nearly all the religious groups in the country met in New York approximately 2 years ago and suggested the 20 cities that would be most crucial for a program of urban seminars. They included Boston, suburban New York City, Washington, Cleveland, Columbus, St. Louis,

Lake County (outside of Chicago), Denver, San Francisco, Los Angeles, San Diego, and New Orleans.

"The urban seminars were university based; i. e., the local university acted as a sponsor and usually provided the major part of the leadership. In a number of cases these urban seminars provided the first opportunity for the leaders of a metropolis to work together on a community level. Many clergymen discovered that they had restricted their work too frequently to the level of community symptoms. The universities in turn gained an appreciation for the role of the church in the local community. In given cases this insight regarding the role of the local church was absolutely astounding to them. The seminars were envisaged for the entire religious community — Protestant, Roman Catholic, Jewish. A high level of cooperation by the three religious communities was experienced in most localities."

The whole world is today moving with fantastic speed into a global urban culture. Beyond metropolis and megalopolis there looms what not churchmen but city planners are already calling "ecumenopolis" — the whole world become one vast interdependent city. The church of Jesus Christ must learn to encounter, cope with, and proclaim the Gospel to urban man. In the process of adjusting the forms of the church to this drastically new situation it will be difficult for the churches of any denomination to find a more knowledgeable and balanced guide than the theologian-sociologist who has prepared these thoughtful and stimulating chapters.

Christmas Eve, 1965   WILLIAM J. DANKER

Tomorrow Emerging Today

The sketches of tomorrow are virtually limitless. They range in depth, style, and mood. George Orwell paints a verbal picture of planned conformity by 1984 that reads like a nightmare. Joseph Wood Krutch takes the measure of man and warns of the "Grand Strategy" trap. Each exhibitor at the New York World's Fair tried to outdo his competitor in portraying the mental and technological advances which lie just beyond tomorrow. Christian leaders also have attempted to peer into the future. Chad Walsh wrote *Early Christians of the 21st Century*. Fifteen years later Harvey Cox portrays *The Secular City,* a theological perspective on secularization and urbanization.[1]

Those focusing on the technological are ecstatic. Space travel. Cities under the sea. Conquest of disease. Automated production through computers. Education with machine learning. A civilization built for the first time to the true scale of man. Those focusing on the social and spiritual dimensions of the future express concern. Some are frightened by minor demons such as boredom. They picture the woman of tomorrow in her gleaming, pastel kitchen, clean and sterile, perfect in design, with piped stereophonic music in the background, talking on her color-picture telephone to a friend while the family's dinner is automatically prepared from the freezer in 4 minutes. They fear that life might become dull in such a setting.

Krutch and others fear bigger demons – the control of men's minds through conditioning. They are afraid of what the social sciences can do when applied to human manipulation. An indication is found in a fantasy like *Walden Two*.[2] Walden Two is a utopian community where people have voluntarily committed themselves. There an experimental psychologist uses techniques for controlling thought with such precision that he produces a group of people who are happy, obedient, and incapable of antisocial behavior. The conditioned reflex takes the place of conscious, often imperfect thought and action.

The theologians are fearful of the greatest demons – those that arise when God and man have died. Johannes C. Hoekendijk, former professor of modern church history at the University of Utrecht, now professor of missions at Union Theological Seminary in New York, indicates why people suggest that only pessimists look into the future. In a provocative article written in 1961 he said that the central theme of tomorrow seems to be fixed: "Man is dead."[3] The variations on the theme are multiple; the theme is unchanged. Consider the contrast. The daring prophets of the 19th century proclaimed: "God is dead!" They did this with passion or pathos, with anger or sorrow; but they did it from mountaintop with trumpet blast. Terrified, mankind fought back or composed great funeral liturgies and dirges. But our 20th-century awareness is not proclaimed. We casually mention man's death as a bit of conversation. "It is a laconic statement made on the terrace over an aperitif; a fragment of boulevard philosophy: 'Man is dead – anybody got a cigarette?'"

When we therefore view the role and shape of the church in the world of tomorrow, we must not foreshorten our question to one that seeks simply to know how the church might reshape itself in modern form to carry on traditional tasks – as if it really remains the same and only a few bits of hardware have been changed. We are dealing with fundamental shifts in our mental world, our social world, our scientific world, our world of art, and our world of religion. Without this awareness we continue to ask the wrong questions. We ask how to patch the old cloth when there is need for a new garment.

I. THE TASK OF UNLEARNING

The greatest breakthrough we need is the acknowledgment that some of our guiding concepts and assumptions in our culture are in serious need of reexamination. With enthusiasm we embrace the new products of technology. In spite of dire predictions of dangers that lurk in the future, most people believe in progress; they assume that the lives of their children will be richer than theirs simply because of the passage of time. We complain where parts of the culture are out of balance — when the production of cars outruns our planning for adequate movement of traffic in our cities. We are bewildered when the clash lies in an area where the moral judgment is more obvious. Decisions in the area of sex morality, child rearing, and the use of power in effecting social change are prime examples.

Beneath the obvious change on the technological level, then, lies a far more consequential change on the level of our thoughts, values, and beliefs. Technological learning can be effected quite easily. A society can readily import technology from another culture. But change on the level of our opinions and guiding concepts is more difficult to analyze with precision. Because of their emotional rootage it is difficult for us to examine them objectively even as we acknowledge need for this process. It is difficult for man to change his perceptions. It takes a degree of objectivity and detachment even to be conscious of this level of concept. As someone has suggested, it would be virtually impossible to get a fish to understand that he is in water. Most of our guiding assumptions have become part of the unchallenged world in which we live.

From his creation God granted man a freedom that he did not give to other created orders within our world. Animals were bound to the natural world. They had to adapt to nature or die. Those species which did not adapt disappeared. But mankind

3

remained plastic. He was granted dominion over the natural world. The great result of this gift of God was the development of a symbolic, cultural world. Through this man was able to transcend his bonds to the world. Like the rest of animal creation, he was bound to the world in his dependence on it for food, shelter protection, and procreation. Human life, however, was planned by the Creator to be more than biological. To handle basic biological problems, man developed a symbolic, cultural life to control and transform both the world and himself. To handle the basic needs of food and shelter, he learned to control and manipulate nature. Within the broad orders of creation that God built into our world, man developed ways of controlling himself and his impulses. Patterns of regulating sex and procreation developed in the sphere of family life; patterns of governing personal and social relationships developed through the state; patterns of providing food and tools developed through forms of economic orders; patterns of response to the Creator and responsibility to His world were developed within the order of the religious community.

Beneath this development man faced four questions. They must be answered again in our day:

1. *What is the nature of the universe?*

Is it rational, benevolent, or strictly mechanical in response? Is all of it moving toward some end? If so, what is the nature of this movement?

2. *What is man's place in the universe?*

Is he the end of all creation? Are there other forms of higher intelligence in the universe?

3. *What is man's relationship to the group?*

Is the individual or the collective of greater worth? In case of necessity, who is sacrificed for whom? How are the individual's own impulses regulated in the light of the group?

4. *What is human nature and conduct?*

What is it to be a man? To what extent is he bound to or liberated from his biological impulses? How is he to perceive his actions and aspirations?

4

Between man and the universe, therefore, lies the level of his symbols. These concepts tell him how to interpret and organize his feelings about and reactions to the universe. They give meaning and purpose to his life. But this symbolic, cultural world is not the same for all men. Symbols are not divinely given; they are human products. They emerge and serve for a time. As human understanding grows, they become antiquated and in need of replacement. Since, however, symbols form part of the building blocks of our thoughts — in the very words, concepts, and syntax we use — change comes very slowly. This provides for cultural continuity. But it also makes for difficulty when people begin to live lives that are liberated from a given concept — while paying emotional obedience to it.

Consider a case in contemporary life where this process has moved far: in our concept of determining guilt and innocence. As humans we have moved through stages where the norm for determining guilt was trial by combat or trial by ordeal. When our culture found that these means no longer produced the desired result, a new social invention was devised: trial by jury. It was felt that a group of one's peers would be in the best position to determine whether or not a man was telling the truth. Important in this process was the oath. The accused man swore that he would tell the truth. All believed that if he failed to do this, he would be punished either immediately or finally on Judgment Day. Today few take the oath seriously. The jury is made up of people who do not know the defendant. In most cases they must decide who is lying the least rather than who is telling the truth.

The continued spread of deep social problems, a growing public sense of confusion and bewilderment, the inability of government on all levels and the host of private agencies to effect more than a momentary diverting of these problems are indications of the growing obsolescence and increasing anachronisms of the basic answers we have been giving to the questions of our personal and corporate life. The need is for more than revamped legislation or even the focusing of a sizable segment of our national concern on aid to a particular deprived sector of our people. The need is for a total reexamination of the concepts that are the tools we use as we think about man, society, and the church.

Frequently it is hard to accept the new. This is particularly so when the new demands a rupture with the beloved and idealized past. The need to which we are calling ourselves, then, is to the task of *unlearning*. We must discard many formulations and guiding concepts that served our forefathers admirably but are no longer useful mental constructs in our day. The founding fathers of our nation, for example, were able to use the assumptions and concepts of the 18th century. These concepts, applied to the social and political realm, were derived in large measure from the world view — the physics — of Newton and Descartes. The models they proposed released an immense amount of energy in building our nation into what it is today.

The founding fathers were forced to a creative task because of the inadequacy of concepts which failed to describe the vision of society that they were proposing. In precisely the same fashion the social concepts of the 18th century — of men like Locke and Berkeley — are inadequate to articulate the vision of man and society which we have caught in our day. Those who would bind us to the past through an appeal for loyalty to our forefathers and their ideas fail to understand that true loyalty to our heritage forces us to be as critical of the meaning of the past to our day as they were in theirs.

The purely rational, mechanical view of man and the universe which comes from an earlier day is inadequate. As a result of the seminal work of Freud and vast research in the social sciences, we now have an understanding of the *ir*rational motivations in life that invalidates the former view. The economic theories of Adam Smith built on an economy of agriculture and scarcity fail to answer the questions of our contemporary social order. In one discipline after another the older mechanistic concepts are out of joint with our modern needs. The potential for developing a model to view the social order today, utilizing the new science of cybernetics and general systems

6

theory, appears promising. To make progress, however, people must agree that a social system does not fall full-blown from heaven but is hammered out in our world. When this is granted, we can conceptualize a social order that is self-governing, self-regulating, and self-renewing.

Lawrence Frank continues to insist on the necessity of this Promethean task. Calling for a restatement of our national aspirations, he said:

> Concretely, this means restating our traditional 'aspirations and redefining our enduring goal values in terms that are appropriate to the needs and the possibilities of today and tomorrow as contrasted with those which were addressed to the needs of a new and largely agricultural nation with a relatively homogeneous population deriving from the same cultural background. Such a restatement will recognize the great promise and also the many hazards of the coming technological advances and the application of automation and will explicitly recognize the new sensibilities and the awakening conscience of the American people, especially the longings and hopes of millions, who came here from other lands and many of whom have been denied full participation in our national life.[4]

As Frank has called for fundamental reexamination in human conservation and has shown its implications for national planning, so we call for such a radical reexamination of our guiding concepts within the church. Such an invitation is pleasantly received so long as it remains a refreshing invitation to look at familiar material from a slightly new point of view. The guarantee must be given, however, that the final product will not be too radical. New slants on the status quo are appreciated. We continue to prove that as a group we are too insecure to venture into the more basic job. Our slogans sound dramatic calls to march into new lands. Somehow, after much marching, we always manage to camp reasonably close to where we began. Hoekendijk reminds us of the widespread conspiracy to leave everything as it is; above all, of our ability to mark time while convincing ourselves that we are moving. He quips about the ingenious invention of an "American egghead" who every day

7

took off in his plane, setting his course so that he would land precisely where he landed the day before.

To clarify some of the unlearning which must take place as tomorrow emerges, we select several factors from the sphere of society and church. Our list is suggestive rather than complete, and the usual classifications of cause and effect will quickly become blurred. We must look at this list, then, as a kaleidoscopic flash of causes compelling the church to examine its need for new shapes if it will be faithful to God and of service to mankind in tomorrow's world.

II. EMERGING NEEDS IN SOCIETY

A. ALIENATION

One of the most anguished cries arising from contemporary society is the cry of alienation. Some speak of anomie, emphasizing our condition of normlessness with the collapse of traditional wisdom and its specific rules of conduct. Novelists, poets, sociologists, psychiatrists — all are concerned with this phenomenon, which shows itself in a tragic sense of loss of self, powerlessness, meaninglessness, depersonalization, and loss of one's beliefs. Those who have analyzed alienation most carefully are impressed with its pervasive quality.[5] Erich Fromm said: "Alienation as we find it in modern society is almost total; it pervades the relationship of man to his work, to the things he consumes, to his fellows, and to himself."

This phenomenon began in our Western world after the great technological and political revolutions of the 18th century. Man freed himself from the rigidity of the former social order; but in doing so, he cut himself adrift from his former roots in a world of stable relationships. Modern man often is estranged from himself as well as from other people. He feels lost. Unable to give the old answers to the four questions we raised earlier regarding the nature of the universe and his personal and corporate relationship to it, man has failed to formulate a new set of answers that appear to have any sanctions for him. Karl Jaspers questions whether man can preserve his selfhood and identity in a world dominated by mass technology and bureau-

8

cratization. He now feels alien before the very world he has created. Somehow the positions of creator and created, subject and object have become confused in a demonic fashion. Is this intense sense of anxiety the price that modern man must pay for progress?

Alienation is more than a personal reaction to a changed world. It has serious social overtones. If the social psychologists are right in their belief that a person acquires his sense of identity through interaction with others, then a person cut off from this interaction through a sense of alienation is cut off from developing his own sense of identity and creativity. Cut off from meaningful contact with the group, he is unable to make a significant social contribution.

But isn't estrangement part of the human problem that men of every age have wrestled with? Were there not equivalent manifestations of this in Egypt 4,000 years ago? in Greece 2,400 years ago? in central Europe 400 years ago? Indeed there always are individuals alienated from the group. But in each of these earlier periods there were strong unified groups into which a person was born. In medieval Europe existence demanded attachment to a particular group—a household, a guild, a monastery, or a band of robbers. Security lay only in association. With the breakup of the feudal caste system, the individual arose as the significant unit of society rather than the group. Coupled with this was a vast increase of his power over nature, culminating in the industrial revolution. Each step further served to cut off his rootage in family, group, and the natural world. Man alone arose. But he was a man given to self-conscious awareness of his new state—one of growing estrangement from all created things about him.

B. WORK—AUTOMATION—LEISURE

The complex of work and leisure is the second area to which our emerging shapes of the church must give answer. The church has interpreted the field of work and production as one of the "orders" which God has given to rule the world. Work is part of God's design. It was part of His plan for mankind even

9

prior to the Fall. Thus it is not a result of sin. It is a means through which a man provides his own food and shelter, serves as a caretaker of God's world, and serves other people.

But the vast changes in our culture have greatly affected the world of work. For many today the sole purpose of work lies in the consumption which their wages make possible. So often there is little conscious decision to enter a specific line of work. Most assembly-line workers accepted a job that was open when their schooling finished. Years later they have built up a degree of security in their job which keeps them there. Since the job itself is not significant, since most workers do not speak highly of their contacts with fellow workers, and since most are not too conscious of how their particular process relates to the eventual finished product, the goal becomes one of getting as much money as possible for as few hours as possible spent in the least boring and tiring way possible.

Relatively few people in our society are actually involved in making products. Most of us are several steps removed from the actual "thing." We deal with paper—with plans and administration. If forced to analyze the whole process rationally, we would admit that perhaps the majority of men do not do "useful" work. Planned obsolescence, bureaucratic procedures, and commodities of questionable social value place many people in the tragic plight of finding meaning in their work only in terms of what happens outside of work.

A half generation ago the major concern was with the depersonalization that resulted from a man's being tied to a machine which dictated the rhythm of his life. In the intervening years a revolution in production has taken place which appears to be of as great significance as was the industrial revolution. We are approaching the day when perhaps 3 percent of the population together with machines will be able to produce all of the goods our society can use. Already we have entered the day when the doors of industry are closed to those who have only a strong back and hands to offer. Quickly the process advances to include more highly skilled blue- and white-collar workers. At the present time many middle-management jobs are

10

much more highly structured because many decisions once made by such levels of men are now being programed by machine. While a great number of people currently are moving into service-type occupations, as fabrication of more products permits replacement more cheaply than repair or cleaning, even this field may be sharply curtailed.

Thus the world of leisure—desired or enforced through unemployment—becomes a challenge to the church. In the foreseeable future, work will continue to decline as a central activity, even while many continue to work hard. Current studies of work and leisure have documented the fact that the current urban worker has "advanced" to the point where he has as much leisure as did his counterpart in the 13th century. Many who have gained a shorter workweek have simply taken on a second job in order to increase their ability to consume. But for more people leisure has become a desperate escape from work which they find relatively meaningless. The challenge is to use in a constructive way the time that has been freed from the tasks of providing for physical needs. Leisure and recreation can become more than mass activities and packaged entertainment. In its concern with the total life of man, the church has an opportunity to be of genuine service in working with people in shaping their values and patterning their lives in a world where leisure replaces the central role of work.[6]

C. URBANIZATION

Closely related to the foregoing and at times overlapping are the challenges emerging from our urbanized world. There is no longer any need for documenting the emergence of our urban civilization. Its implications surround us. We do need, however, to sense its theological dimensions. Living in a culture that has developed amid a deep distrust of the city—in which the pious has been equated with the rural—we need to see minimally that environment is neutral. It can be a creative, beneficial setting, or it can be the means of releasing destructive influences. God remains Lord of the city also. In His wisdom He is permitting the growth of monster cities through-

11

out the world. To carry out our mission, we need to examine our tasks in terms of His will for man, society, and the world in the setting of an urban society.

The world of the city is a mosaic of individuals and sub-groups which may have little personal relationship. In place of total involvement with other persons, people interact segmentally in prescribed roles. The individual often feels alone; in fact he may be quite powerless. Because of diversity of backgrounds and value systems he finds himself confused about what is right. Morality seems to break down because the crowd becomes the moral arbiter. Further, the personal ethic learned by the individual becomes confused when it is translated into the public sphere of business or political life.

The world of the city is a stratified society that covers the broad continuum from the opulently wealthy to the financially and socially dispossessed. There is relatively little significant interaction among the social classes. One's family, income, occupation, education, and style of life sharply separate him from other people. Thus the affluent live in situations where they meet little hard-core poverty face to face. The aged poor, the minority group, those with inadequate education, those whose technological skills have become obsolete — all face pressures hardly imagined by those who are successful in today's urban society. The Christian is to be different. He does not reach out to those in other social worlds with feelings of superiority or condescension. Seeing God at work in His total creation, he seeks only to bring understanding and healing.[7]

III. EMERGING NEEDS WITHIN THE CHURCH
A. DECLINE OF RELIGION?

It is difficult to assess the role and influence of religion in the West. On the one hand there are those who would see as the central fact of modern history in the West — that is, from the close of the Middle Ages to the present — the unquestionable decline of religion. On the other hand there is the unmistakable fact of the religious revival of the last decade and the continued popularity and strength of churches in North America. Beneath the surface one has even greater difficulty in evaluating the influence of religion in our culture. Most difficult for the Christian is to distinguish the point at which the Christian faith which he affirms has nothing in common with "religion" as such.

Most of us would agree that when our day is compared with the medieval age, religion no longer is the controlling center of man's life. For the medieval man, religion was not an isolated theological system to which he subscribed but, in the words of William Barrett, "a solid psychological matrix surrounding the individual's life from birth to death." Its symbols as well as its dogmas, its images as well as its rites were an inescapable part of his daily life. The Renaissance began a process of stripping the Western mind of these symbols and a psychological dependence on them. The world of faith and a universe inaccessible to human reason was slowly transformed into a realm of neutral objects that could be explained and manipulated through scientific method.

While admitting this fundamental change, the most recent sociological investigations describe our culture as still heavily under the influence of religion. Part of the difficulty is taken care of if we utilize Gerhard Lenski's distinction between communal and associational.[8] For Lenski found, contrary to the expectations of the 19th-century positivists, religious organizations remain vigorous and influential in contemporary American society. If associational aspects of a religious group refer to membership in the church, its communal aspects refer to the ways in which its values, beliefs, and practices are carried by family, friends, and neighborhood interaction. For any given religious group the associational ties may be weak while the communal ties may remain strong. Sociologically, however, most signs in our society point to expected gains in associational vigor in the foreseeable future. Changes in American society are strengthening and enlarging those groups—for example, third-generation Americans and middle-class people—which historically have been the strongest supporters of churches.

13

Sociologists who made community studies were informally agreed several years ago that one could gain an understanding of an entire community without examining its religious groups. These were considered exclusivistic with no influence on the community itself. Some of the more overt types of religious participation in areas such as the civil-rights movement have caused them to reexamine their position. Under closer scrutiny they have come to sense the interweaving of religion into virtually every area of a community's life.

B. PLURALISM

The second ingredient in our culture that is posing particular problems for churches is the fact of pluralism. For the first half of the religious and cultural history of the United States, life was dominated by the Protestant state churches. With the breakup of the colonial state churches, there followed a period which Littell aptly describes as one of voluntaryism.[9] During this period the churches attempted to win people back into membership. The emphasis was on mass evangelism and revivalism. It was during this second period that the nation received large influxes of immigrants of Roman Catholic, Jewish, and Orthodox backgrounds. We are currently in a third period, with a style of church life characterized by openness and dialog. Structures and outlooks appropriate to an earlier day are being reexamined. The relationship of the churches to the whole public sphere — particularly their relationship to political structures — is undergoing change. Dialogs among churches are proceeding on several levels simultaneously.

This challenge is particularly troublesome because churchmen are having difficulty in clarifying their values and in keeping their practice in conformity with their theological tenets. Men are struggling to find a *modus operandi* by which they will be able to have the conviction to remain forthright confessional churchmen and at the same time be sympathetic and brotherly to those who are loyal sons of totally divergent theological traditions. Obviously our contemporary structures

14

will reflect both our theological heritage and our newly sharpened awareness.

C. CALL TO SECULARITY AND SERVICE

Churchmen today feel called by God to a relevant contact with the world. While their fathers in their concern for doctrinal and ecclesiastical purity tended to withdraw from the world, their sons are plunging into involvement with the life of the world at every point possible. Pastors are resigning conventional pastorates to attach themselves to the jazz community in New York, to the homosexual community in San Francisco, to the civil-rights movement in Chicago. Their driving desire is to bring the Gospel to those who have conventionally felt cut off from the typical middle-class congregation. They take seriously the work of God in all of His creation, especially where He is at work apart from the organized church.[10]

Their call to secularity is to be distinguished from an easy accommodation to secularism — although at times the border line is hard to define. They do not seek a freedom to live as pagans in the world; they know the freedom to plunge knowingly into the secular world in an effort to bring to it a knowledge of God, its Creator, Judge, and Redeemer. They have learned to listen and to learn from the world before they speak and judge. Because of this sensitivity they fall prey to the danger of removing all judgment from their ministry. For support and correction they need strong contacts with their fellow believers.

Further, the contemporary church in living with the world has become sensitive to a need to serve the world — particularly those who have been forced to the perimeter of our society, those dispossessed from the riches and goods of our culture. Having heard the cry of anguish from the suffering, they can never again live amid the affluence of the organizational church without using their lives in personal and professional service. For them service never again can become a pleasant "extra" for those within the church inclined to be interested in such under-

15

takings; it is part of the heart of the church's whole ministry to mankind.

Because of the speed of change, tomorrow is emerging today. Amid dire predictions that we are living in a post-Christian period when secularism has succeeded the Faith, men survey the future to discover whether it will be a desert — a Christian wasteland — or the setting for a vitality of the Faith-within-life such as our world has not seen for 700 years. The changes demanded by the future involve more than slight shifts of technique. They demand a fundamental review of the great concepts which guide our thinking and acting. This involves unlearning. Then looking realistically at our emerging world of technology and urbanization, we ask how the people of God can shape their witness most effectively in a world where the role of religion has been in historical decline and in a time when consciousness of pluralism is strong. They are still called to a ministry of proclamation and service. Desert or promised land — we move ahead with courage and joy, for we move under His blessing.

NOTES FOR CHAPTER I

[1] Joseph Wood Krutch, *The Measure of Man* (New York: Charter Books, 1953); Chad Walsh, *Early Christians of the 21st Century* (New York: Harper, 1950); Harvey Cox, *The Secular City* (New York: The Macmillan Co., 1965).

[2] Burrhus F. Skinner, *Walden Two* (New York: The Macmillan Co., 1948 [Paperback ed., 1962]).

[3] Johannes C. Hoekendijk, "On the Way to the World of Tomorrow," *Laity,* No. 11 (August 1961), pp. 5 – 19.

[4] From an unpublished paper, "Human Conservation — The Democratic Task" (A Statement Prepared for United Planning Organization, Washington, D. C., n. d.), p. 5.

[5] Erich Fromm, *The Sane Society* (New York: Rinehart, 1955); Karl Jaspers, *Man in the Modern Age* (Garden City, N. Y.: Doubleday Anchor Books, 1957). For an excellent selection of articles on modern alienation, see Eric and Mary Josephson, eds., *Man Alone: Alienation in Modern Society* (New York: Dell Publishing Co. [A Laurel Edition] 1962).

[6] See Hugh C. White, Jr., ed., *Christians in a Technological Era* (New York: The Seabury Press, 1964).

[7] For a useful sampling of thought regarding our urban civilization, see C. E. Elias, Jr., James Gillies, and Svend Riemer, eds., *Metropolis: Values in Conflict* (Belmont, Calif.: Wadsworth Publishing Co., 1964).

16

[8] Gerhard Lenski, *The Religious Factor* (Garden City, N. Y.: Doubleday, 1961), pp. 10–11, 33–39.

[9] Franklin H. Littell, *From State Church to Pluralism* (Garden City, N. Y.: Doubleday Anchor Books, 1962). Cf. Chs. I and II.

[10] Among the more articulate American spokesmen Peter Berger and Gibson Winter particularly stand out. Cf. Peter L. Berger, *The Noise of Solemn Assemblies* (Garden City, N. Y.: Doubleday, 1961); Gibson Winter, *The New Creation as Metropolis* (New York: The Macmillan Co., 1963).

2

Emerging Shapes of Personal Life

The emerging world of tomorrow is molding the life of people individually and collectively. We may rejoice in the effects or draw back convinced that the changes we behold are demonic. The first level of change does not lie with the group but deals with the individual.

Whenever we are tempted to talk about "modern man" in sweeping generalizations of any variety, it is useful to become precise regarding the points at which we are dealing with "human" problems—those facing man in any generation—over against those which are "modern"—new or at least highly intensified in our day.

I. VIEWING MODERN MAN

When Emil Brunner addressed himself to the theme "The Word of God and Modern Man"[1] in the late forties, he found it necessary first to develop the basic point that modern man is first and foremost *man*. We must face the fixed qualities of man, his creatureliness, his dependence on God—whether recognized or not—his ultimate responsibility as a creature. He is not autonomous; he is not a god; he can be understood only in relationship. Therefore the real depth of his problems eludes crass oversimplification which reduces him to animal existence, a stomach, a brain, or a set of sex organs. And although psychiatry, sociology, and biology are highly helpful, they remain partial disciplines that can describe but one segment of the whole reality of man.

Modern man is fundamentally and foremost *man*. But even his basic creatureliness is seen in a particular way in our day. To say that man is a creature is to say that he is not divine; he is not a god. But any sensitivity to the modern temper leads one to realize that this is not modern man's temptation. Men in other ages were tempted to stand as Titans, ready to assault the heights of heaven and proclaim themselves gods. But strangely enough, when man reached the highest point in his scientific exploration and projected a future in which his science and technology would dwarf even the new frontiers of tomorrow, he felt less God-like than ever in his history. From the lips of his poets and dramatists there issues the anguished cry of nothingness.[2] He can think of himself as an animal. He can feel himself a nonentity in the vastness of the cosmos. He despairs to find meaning in his life; the greater tragedy is to know that even his death will count for nothing. "A soldier with no zest for fighting, a poet with no zeal for writing, an architect without a plan; the prototype of modern man." So John Cooper has described his condition.

Sigmund Freud once delineated the three deathblows delivered to man's sense of worth and significance.[3] The first blow was the cosmological one, struck by Copernicus, when man was forced to acknowledge that the earth, far from the center of the universe, was little more than a bit of cosmic dust. The second blow was biological, struck by Charles Darwin when he further showed man that he was nothing more than a higher kind of animal. The final blow was psychoanalytical, struck by Freud himself when he showed man to be basically an irrational creature, the pathetic result of storming inner impulses and conflicts.

Modern man remains man, but with an interpretation of the world and himself that has been devastating to his former conceptions. After the three deathblows to his evaluation of himself, where could man turn for salvation? For many modern men religion no longer could serve. Freud had taken special pains to make clear that of the many illusions which tyrannize men because of their neuroses the greatest is religion. The development of every concept of religion from guilt to God he analyzed on the basis of psychoanalytic theory. His conclusion: Religion arises from an immature wish fulfillment; God the Father is a projection into a transcendent realm of our ambivalent feelings of desiring security and affection from our father and yet hating him. The Christian myth of the redemptive death of the Son of God is but a development of the most crass totemism, which Freud sees as the beginning of all religion.

Modern man can achieve rescue from his lost condition by following one of the three roads laid out by Freud, Marx, or Comte. He can be delivered from his neuroses, from his childhood fears and illusions; he can achieve maturity through psychoanalysis. Or he can find meaning in life through a Marxian dialectic. History then does have meaning; man's life can count in the great struggle between the classes. A classless society will emerge in which conflict among men will be forever gone. Those analyses of communism which are most perceptive understand it as a predestinarian *religious* movement! Its theology, its call to discipleship, its offer of meaning in life still enlist many.

Auguste Comte, the French philosopher who is considered the father of sociology, might stand as the symbol for a third route of salvation. For Comte also religion stands as a milestone in humanity's long march toward progress. He divided human history into three stages: the theological, in which men relied on spirits and gods; the metaphysical, in which they relied on philosophy; and the positivistic, in which men will be freed through the use of empirical science. In the latter years of his life he developed a missionary zeal in enlisting people to work toward the ultimate perfect society in a humanistic type of "religion of humanity."

Modern man, we are saying, maintains his continuity with man. Because he views his world so differently and because he is offered a new set of saviors, we need to see him in the light of several Scriptural affirmations. While modern man will accept one aspect of his creatureliness — dust of the dust — his limited, dependent situation in the universe, he balks before a second affirmation: he is created in the image of God. He is the loving and special creation from the hand of God. He is not independent. While dependent on God, he is given a degree of freedom no other creature has. He is to respond to God freely. God made man to be a son — to know a free response of love. His self-determination has limits set by God. But man is free to make decisions — to live responsibly before God. Man is made in the image of God. This means, as Luther saw so simply yet so profoundly, that man was made to live in fellowship with God, to live in faith and love. And this is a gift bestowed by God.

Modern man is more likely to understand the third Biblical description of man: he is a sinner. Made in the image of God, it is true, but rebellious and idolatrous. Faith is wrenched from its moorings in God and turned upside down to become sin. The life of man now bears an inner contradiction. The perversion of faith and love shows in all of man's relationships. A perversion takes place in man's relationship to the Creator, to himself, and to other creatures. Sin means that man is cut off from God. This lies at the center of all of his other perversions. Man must place his trust in some power; he must worship some god. When estranged from his Creator, he creates gods in his own image. Sin shows further in man's estrangement from himself. Modern man is hauntingly aware of this fact. Because of the inner contradiction of having a destiny planned by God and now cut loose from it, man lives a life with no clear and fulfilling purpose. Although modern man denies any absolutes, he is torn between the tension of an "oughtness" which he feels and the reality of his disobedience, which creates an undefined anxiety. Our generation recognizes the dimension of sin as a disruption of relationships among people. Self-love and the will to power have been seen in their sheer ugliness in our generation. Middle-class gentility has proved to be a thin veneer over a harsh nature which seeks the good primarily for self. Even while speaking the language of "I—thou," so many moderns have been subtly maneuvering for positions of dominance. Within our heart of hearts, as Brunner comments, we are forced to confess that we have loved ourselves with all our heart and with all our soul and with all our power; we are neighbors to ourselves.

The final Biblical accent we need for understanding man is to hear again that he is redeemed. God remains God. God acts. God loves. God enters the arena of human life to reestablish a relationship with rebellious mankind. In His Son God effects the change which makes possible a new creation. God was in Christ reconciling the world to Himself. Christ took the sin of humanity upon Himself and in the fires of Golgotha purified a new humanity. Because of God's intervention the power of sin is broken; death is defeated; sin is forgiven; and life has hope. Man now can look toward tomorrow without experiencing the final despair that is the concomitant of death.

To understand modern man, we must see his continuity with all men. We have already implied, however, that there are specific points at which the modern situation has intensified the problem of man's unbelief. At the heart of this changed condition lies modern man's deliberate, conscious declaration of liberation from God. For some this takes the form of denying any god who is more than the synthesis of the highest values held among people. God is little more than the personification of the highest spirit of love among people. Among others there is simply an ignoring of God. In facing some of the most significant decisions of life, people find that God plays no direct, observable role. No question is asked to which God is the answer. Many fling a defiant challenge of freedom from God in the area of morality. They are independent, they insist, of any of God's laws. They acknowledge no divine authority that is binding on them. They declare their unconditional freedom from any Creator. This modern attitude has been in formation over a long period of time. Most historians of culture would plot the beginning of this attitude in the Renaissance. But that which was tacitly agreed to has now been consciously articulated and made the declaration of a generation.

The corollary to modern man's demand for autonomy is his rejection of any concept of revelation. Even for those who speak favorably of Christianity's contribution to modern culture or defend the necessity of "religion," the concept of revelation usually stands as an offense. God is not found through His self-disclosure; He is to be discovered through the eclectic process of surveying the whole sphere of the world's great religions and selecting the values and insights which have greatest significance for the individual today. In fairness one must grant that what the modern man rejects is often a caricature of the Biblical picture of revelation. Nevertheless, there is a repudiation of any God who holds concourse with man in order to reveal Himself to him.

Modern man then emerges as one who emphasizes his emancipation from God, who is less inclined to proclaim himself a god than he is to denigrate himself to the level of animality or futility, who stands offended before a God who claims to reveal Himself to humanity, who in freedom has discovered anguish but is unable to find salvation in God. As Christians we live in the midst of the culture which has produced these attitudes. It is well to reflect on how deeply these same attitudes have etched themselves into the core of our lives.

II. THE PROBLEM OF BELIEF IN GOD

Nowhere does this new mind-set show itself more clearly than in the central question: Can modern man still believe in the type of God revealed in the Bible? This is usually phrased: Can we still believe in a "God out there"? The well-known answer of John A. T. Robinson, who has popularized several continental and American theologians — primarily Dietrich Bonhoeffer and Paul Tillich — is: "No!"

In his published lecture "Can a Truly Contemporary Person *Not* Be an Atheist?"[4] he summarizes the three motives that have impelled men over the last three centuries to question their belief in God: God is intellectually superfluous; God is emotionally dispensable; God is morally intolerable.

He recapitulates Bonhoeffer's argument that God is no longer used to fill the gaps in our knowledge in the fields of science, art, or technology. Thus to explain facts that are still beyond human explanation with the answer of "God" is an act of intellectual laziness or practical superstition. Within the last century it has also become true of religion, Robinson claims, that one can get along without "God." In our world come-of-age, Christian apologists try to secure an area where God still can furnish the answer to the ultimate questions of death and guilt. But, they ask, what will happen when also these questions can be answered without the hypothesis of God? Robinson concludes his first argument:

> Most of us today are practical atheists. The "god-hypothesis" is as irrelevant for running an economy or coping with the population explosion as it was for Laplace's system. As a factor you must take into account in the practical business of living, God is "out" — and no amount of religious manipulation can force Him back in. He is peripheral, redundant, incredible — and therefore *as God* displaced: in Julian Huxley's words, "not a ruler, but the last fading smile of a cosmic Cheshire Cat."[5]

Robinson's second argument, that man no longer needs God emotionally, builds on the Freudian argument that religion is but a symptom of emotional immaturity. When God is seen as a projection of men's fears and anxieties, then it is a sign of health and maturity to "grow up and shake off the sense of helplessness which religion both induces and sanctions." With others he calls for people to accept the emerging secular world responsibly and not project ultimate responsibility upon spirits in some other world. His total argument is less crass than this brief condensation suggests. The heart of his argument is Bonhoeffer's concern: Until we rid ourselves of the "God of religion," we will never understand what Jesus is showing us from the cross.

25

His final argument for 20th-century atheism articulates the problem of suffering and evil which one finds in Camus and Sartre. In the words of a 19-year-old girl who was asked whether she believed in God: "I don't see how there can be a benevolent God. There are too many tragedies – personal and in the world. . . . Religion is disgusting." One can no longer calmly accept, Robinson argues, the 16th-century view of disease and accident as sent by God – without portraying Him as demonic. Further, men must stand erect and face their responsibility in meeting tragedy and not place the blame on the shoulders of a mythical being.

But what do we do after the death of God? After people admit the validity of the atheist's arguments, after they have gone through the valley of unbelief – what? Most discover they cannot remain atheists. Though they may want to reject God, "yet, in grace and demand, he *will not* let us go. The hound of heaven still dogs us, the 'beyond in our midst' still encounters us when all the images, all the projections, even all the words, for God have been broken." After the death of God, these insist, you still find Him disturbingly alive. The traditional pictures of God are for the most part destroyed, but the reality of God – whatever the image – exists. He may come through the claims of artistic or scientific truth, through involvement with social justice or personal fellowship. One knows that it is God whom he is meeting because He comes with an "over-mastering givenness and demand" such as no person or idea has the right or power to convey or require. Robinson refers to this as a "post-resurrection" world: the old is dead; when *we* no longer need God emotionally, when we reject the curtailing of laws, we find the Lord appearing to us alive.

Regardless of our first emotional reactions to this line of thought, one is forced to admit that these men within the church are interpreting the voices of people outside. Obviously they are speaking for many intellectuals, but one senses that they are also voicing part of what the uneducated man feels deep within him. Indeed they are not speaking for all. They are forced to acknowledge in turn that within their own thought struc-

26

tures there is a strong residue of the traditional religion from the days of Grandfather.

Our task is not to offer rebuttal but to listen. For some of the emerging structures are attempts to meet the mind-set of this type of person. It is useful, however, to view the responses within the churches to this call for a "religionless Christianity." On the one side are those who see it as the most diabolical scheme to lead people away from God. It is viewed as a reduction of classical Christianity, as apostasy, as a mistaken attempt to accommodate to the thought patterns of the world. On the other side it has been compared to Luther's posting of the Ninety-five Theses – the trumpet call for a 20th-century reformation, an event that has discarded a carload of sterile metaphysical concepts that have too long encumbered the church. Rather than confirming unbelief, proponents of the secular meaning of the Gospel see it as permitting the Easter light to show in its pristine whiteness.

One of the most revealing and troubling experiences of a group of seminary professors and administrators at the Institute for Advanced Pastoral Studies[6] was a discussion with a group of highly intelligent and articulate laymen, virtually all of whom would espouse the Bonhoeffer-Robinson line of thought. On the one hand it was apparent that these individuals were "within the church" only because of the warm acceptance, the liberal theology, and the permissive attitude of the young rector. Several in the group were former agnostics, highly rejective of the church; two still were Buddhists; one was a Jew. They were highly articulate about their absolute disdain of authoritarian views of God; they were most uncomfortable before any exclusive claims for Christianity. But while they were active members of a church, one could not refrain from asking whether they had heard the Gospel of Jesus Christ. This was high humanitarianism, but was it more? Were they speaking a deep theology, as some of the seminary men insisted, in secular terms? Were we doing them an extreme disservice in our attempt to interpret their patterns of thought against a Christological, demand-grace frame of thinking?

27

When we become overly concerned with the difficulties of proclaiming God to our generation, we need the sobering reminder that every age is ultimately an age of unbelief. Intensification of difficulties and new shapes of unbelief, it is true, but ultimately each generation stands offended before the Gospel itself. One can debate whether it is easier to present the Gospel in a culture where the church is protected and revered, where clergymen are given special privilege, where new churches are being built at phenomenal rates, where religion is acknowledged even by the irreligious to be a technique for maintaining values, and where in crisis situations people find themselves superstitiously seeking divine reassurance. Or will the Gospel stand out with greater clarity precisely when the old respectabilities and traditions are thrown over, when people reject concepts of God that are so heavily compounded with folk superstitions that Biblical affirmations are hardly recognizable, where culture and faith are sharply and decisively separated?

III. CHALLENGE IN MORALITY

This change in the basic value system of our day is revealed most dramatically in the argument raging over the so-called "new morality." It must be admitted that this term has been used to cover so broad a field, from serious Christian discussion that appeals for a guiding ethic for the 20th century to defenses of hard-core pornography, that it is virtually worthless as a description of a precise point of view. It is instructive, however, to use the two poles of an "old" and a "new" morality to highlight some of the changes that are taking place.[7]

Three terms might characterize the old morality. It was unchanging; it was authoritative; it dealt with law. Let us look at each point for a moment. The older morality was viewed as an eternally unchanging code. Laws that regulated sex, divorce, or conduct of war were seen as divinely given. Indeed each generation had to make application of the law to its age. But the content was given. "Right" and "wrong" were clearly defined categories which did not change with circumstances. The church was seen as the chief moral agent of society, whose task it was to teach the moral code based on God's divine laws and to guide children and adults into internalizing the code.

Second, the old morality was authoritative. Minimally it had the support and sanction of the culture; maximally it possessed the authority of God Himself. The emphasis was on content: specific principles had been articulated which held sway in every culture. Morality proceeds from a clear set of absolute standards that serve as the touchstone for all time.

Third, the old morality stressed laws. It proceeded from a highly realistic view of human sin. Tolerating no sentimentality about human perfectability, it was concerned with erecting a dike around human existence which kept under careful control the animal and demonic forces within man. Morality needed the power of law to regulate human behavior. Even the Christian who saw himself as part of God's new creation recognized that he, too, lived under law.

In our attempt to simplify the old morality, we hope we have not distorted it. Remaining sympathetic, we recognize the strengths and weaknesses related to this approach. The old morality provided a sure anchor. Regardless of change, it provided a fixed point of reference. By giving morality theological and social roots, the older approach was able to avoid the current modern tendency toward exclusivism. Acts were seen to have social consequences; the individual was responsible to the group. Since its principles were absolute, it also avoided the pitfall of relativism. The old morality withstood the onslaughts of hedonism and the tendency of persons to make the pursuit of their own happiness a chief goal in life.

But the old morality had its weaknesses. Because of its fixed beginning point, a person often was lost in the crush of conflicting principles. Changed circumstances made the application of generalized concepts extremely difficult. When one once takes the pathway of law, he can only continue on the road of casuistry. Each law becomes obsolete the moment it is effected because a new circumstance has arisen not yet covered in the code. Furthermore, it becomes easy to keep the letter of the law while doing violence to its spirit. In this process the motivation of love is continually being squeezed out.

Now the new morality has arisen precisely because of these weaknesses. When the common acceptance of God among intellectuals began to fade and when His direct meaning in life for the man in the street was dulled, any attempt to base morality on divine law became tenuous. The core of common assumptions which supported our moral system and had remained relatively unquestioned began to erode. The general scientific and academic spirit in the land was to question everything. An inherited moral code came in for close scrutiny. The deathblows applied to man's evaluation of himself by Copernicus, Darwin, and Freud had their effects here. Specifically moralistic attitudes were to be avoided in psychoanalysis if the person was to be brought to a higher level of maturity. Anthropology contributed to this questioning of the old morality as it demonstrated the relativity of moral codes across the world. Educationally the philosophy of John Dewey, which emphasized self-determination and self-expression, questioned the judgment of transmitting the content of set moral codes to children. Because of these factors a new moral climate began to develop which approached precisely from the opposite side of the old morality.

The hallmarks of the new morality are its fluidity, its experience orientation, and its love motivation. Whereas the former approach had a tendency to ossify into rigid codes, the new morality underscores the need for freedom and fluidity. The exponents of the new morality point out that in spite of denials to the contrary the content of Christian morality has changed considerably over the centuries. As a spokesman for the new morality, Bishop Robinson indicates the reason for the change: "The raw material of an ethic is provided by the ethos of a society or a century or a group. Times change and even Christians change with them." Therefore new knowledge and changed social or technological conditions would affect and change the content of morals. The only given content for Christian morality is the command to love. Everything else must remain changeable.

The new morality disclaims *absolute* authority and proceeds empirically. The emphasis is on the word "absolute," for it does appeal to authority as found in empirical science. It is fearful of supposed absolute divine authority. Its method is clearly inductive. It begins with the facts of particular experience and then moves to a general understanding. One man writing in defense of this position referred to it as a "morality of involvement and discovery." The argument is that the former absolutes are of little value in our rapidly changing day. Our task, then, is to search out a satisfactory basis for personal and social morality. Christians who make this appeal use the analogy of the Incarnation. Jesus spoke with authority, yet it was an authority which lay concealed behind a complete humanity. The Son of God could be seen only in the Son of Man. People came to see and accept His authority in an inductive fashion. Because it authenticated itself, it demonstrated its reliability.

While the new morality — among Christians at least — makes clear that it is not antinomian, its emphasis is on love rather than law. Jesus' teaching is seen not as a *reform* of Jewish legalism but its *death*. And Jesus presented no new laws to take the place of those which He fulfilled. Thus the Ten Commandments are seen as a false base on which to build a New Testament ethic of love. This love in the new morality does not contradict the older laws, nor does it relieve one from his obligation; but by moving beyond them to the absolute claim of God it destroys them as *law*. As indicated earlier, the new morality summarizes all of Jesus' ethics in an unconditional love of one's neighbor. This is not presented in the form of codes. When illustrations are given in the Gospels to indicate how this new life will show itself, it is demonstrated in an absolute act of love toward the particular neighbor who is there. It is not a carefully articulated code by which men could live. It is rather like the isolated flash of lightning that illumines the night sky for a split second.

Emotions about the new morality run high on both sides of the Atlantic. Frequently the argument has been conducted on the level of slogans. The objective listener wonders whether some are so anxious about their position that they find it virtually impossible to hear what the other is honestly saying. Because of the variety of positions, all of which are vaguely grouped under the single heading of "new morality," it is well to find out whether the speaker is an Anglican bishop, the editor of *Playboy* magazine, or a local hoodlum. The most helpful analyses are those which admit that we need the strengths of each position without their accompanying weaknesses. Thus we find the three emphases we have discussed in necessary working tension. Morality needs both its unchanging quality and its freedom to respond to changed circumstances; it needs authority but must be conscious of the world to which it is addressed; it needs the dikes of laws to restrain sin, but its motivation moves beyond into the area of responsible love. The beginning points remain different, even while one approach moves toward the other.

IV. TOWARD MAKING CONTACT

Our presupposition in this chapter is that if one rushes too quickly into talking about new forms of the church before looking closely at the accompanying changes in people and society, he will do little more than deal with a passing fad. We have attempted to survey some of the qualities that intensify the problems of modern man. Many of his problems are the fundamental problems of humans in any age, but they have received a new form in our day. The outstanding characteristic of modern man is his declaration of independence from God. Many are openly questioning former conceptions of God as inadequate for our day. Others have become practical atheists who don't even bother about the question of God, for God has no relevance to the questions that concern them day by day.

The presuppositions about God which the church of another age could assume have disappeared in more-sophisticated groups and are fast fading in others. In an essay on preaching entitled "New Wine for Fresh Skins," Kent S. Knutson details three presuppositions of yesteryear which have disappeared.[8] Gone is the view of God as the living, sovereign, Holy One of the Bible. A limp "cream puff grandfather who has no fiery sense of community, of the fact that God works with us through in good or evil" has remained where former concepts melted away. The Person of God has disappeared; He has become a formless mask behind history or a personification of love.

The second presupposition that has disappeared is a vital sense of community, of the fact that God works with us through a covenant. In spite of the collectivistic tendencies of our day, people do not look to the church as a vital group of individuals drawn together by God and with whom one is inextricably involved.

Finally, a basic change has occurred in our view of nature and history. The compact world of neat, tight little formulas has exploded. And it takes a greater and greater "leap" of faith to see the hand of God behind contemporary history. "To put it bluntly," Knutson says, "the world has become greater than our picture of God."

An area of vital theology speaks to each of these three changes. Thus they become areas which must concern each man who would preach the Gospel to modern people. In order to avoid inadequate or negative ideas clinging to some conventional theological concepts the first new area has been termed a "theology of response." This attempts to avoid foreshortening the preaching of the Gospel to an initial pronouncement of forgiveness. It further desires to avoid making sanctification a new table of duties related to the Gospel in only the most awkward fashion. The Gospel which brings a man to faith continues to enliven his life of faith and responsible love. This speaks directly to our concerns involved in the new morality.

The second area is called the theology of community. This involves dealing adequately with the doctrine of the laity and the doctrine of the church. We explore this in more detail in the next chapter.

This leaves the doctrine of creation as a response to our new view of the world and history. For to many the doctrine of creation begins and ends with arguments about Genesis 1 – 3. Meanwhile the whole question of the power and lordship of God over all created matter today is sadly neglected. Paul sees the whole of creation involved in redemption. Our day needs to regain the broader conception of the cosmic dimensions of the Atonement as found in the New Testament. The Bible closes with the hope of a new heaven and a new earth; the victory of Christ in His death and resurrection reaches out to all nature. In our open-ended universe this presents the possibility of speaking genuine meaning. For the Spirit still hovers over man with the life and power of God.

NOTES FOR CHAPTER 2

[1] H. Emil Brunner, *The Word of God and Modern Man,* trans. David Cairns (Richmond: John Knox Press, 1964).

[2] For example, Albert Camus' *The Fall* or *The Plague;* T. S. Eliot's *The Waste Land;* Andre Gide's *The Counterfeiters* and *The Immoralist;* William Golding's *Lord of the Flies;* Franz Kafka's *The Trial;* Jean Paul Sartre's *Being and Nothingness.*

[3] Ernest Jones, *The Life and Work of Sigmund Freud,* II (New York: Basic Books, Inc., 1955), 225f.

[4] John A. T. Robinson, *The New Reformation?* (Philadelphia: The Westminster Press, 1965), pp. 106 – 22.

[5] Ibid., p. 109.

[6] A conference for seminary professors on "The Purpose and Process of Theological Education," held in Bloomfield Hills, Mich.; June 21 – 30, 1965.

[7] Cf. John A. T. Robinson, *Christian Morals Today* (Philadelphia: The Westminster Press, 1964).

[8] Kent S. Knutson, "New Wine for Fresh Skins," *Dialog,* III, 1 (Winter 1964), 2 – 47.

3

Emerging Shapes of Community Life

We are struggling to achieve a concept of the church which will dictate the forms that might legitimately arise in the midst of our generation. An illustration of a concept rejected by a growing number of us was afforded by a German missionary from South Africa.[1] In speaking to the Zulus about the church, he used the illustration of their kraal, the thorny hedge enclosure used to fence in their cattle. He pictured the kraal as providing protection. One day a calf smelled the fresh grass on the outside and, not knowing about outside dangers, pushed through the protective thicket and got out. Eventually the entire herd followed. As they scattered, they fell prey to wild animals one by one.

The protected place within the kraal is the church, the Christian congregation. "Remain there," the missionary pleaded. "Don't be tempted by the green grass on the outside. If you stay within the closely knit circle of the congregation, you will be safe in God's keeping." Many preachers in America have similarly urged their people to remain within the kraal. Perhaps even more say this to congregations through the non-verbal language of church programs. We have made the fenced-in area the center of our concern, and most clerical and lay efforts are expended in maintaining the fence. Occasionally another is added to the flock; and we make sure that not too many slip outside. Of late – recognizing the limitations of this approach – some have added cell groups to study about life outside the kraal.

I. THE CHURCH ON MISSION

Throughout the history of the church, however, another dominating concept has jostled the first. This view sees the church as a pilgrim band, as the dispersed church, as the church apostolically sent to the world. In the Epistle to Diognetus we find a classic statement of this view that Christians are not distinguished by their withdrawal from society: "For Christians are distinguished from the rest of mankind neither by country nor by language nor by customs. For nowhere do they dwell in cities of their own; they do not use some different language nor practice an extraordinary kind of life."[2] Instead, the author continued, they live in cities with other men and follow local customs in the usual arrangements of life.

Preachers and popularizers have worked to create a picture that will convey this emphasis to people as clearly as the walled model. Some have suggested a comparison to paratroopers. The church is an army that is scattered to do a job. The group unquestionably needs training; they are gathered and assembled at certain times; they are equipped for their task. But the task is performed as they finally land in enemy territory.

Any sense of a radical quality in the latter description eludes us because we have spoken in this fashion for such a long time. We have discussed the role of the laity until more-active church members squirm uncomfortably when the subject is announced. Sermons regularly berate church members for failing to serve as bearers of the faith to those on the outside. Periodicals are heavy with articles detailing another area of the world where the church has failed to raise an active witness.

These efforts have failed to effect a fundamental change in the style of life of congregations or of individual Christians. While one admits that basic changes are slow in coming, there appear to be additional factors inhibiting this conscious movement of the church out into life through its members. Clergy have failed to do this. Though they have paid lip service to this "ideal," another part of their professional lives sabotaged their words and told people not to take them too seriously. Some pastors unconsciously were threatened professionally. Insecure and unsure of their roles as they were in a rapidly changing culture, this emphasis on laity simply added to their anxiety about their significance and their tasks as pastors. Further, most of them restricted the shift of concept to the point where the laity was expected to become even more active within the kraal, while a few were hesitantly permitted outside the kraal within highly specified limits.

Before we ask about new shapes which various levels of the institutional church might assume, our task is to take the intermediate step of investigating some implications of emerging shapes of community life and potential roles of Christians within them.

II. RAISING SIGNS TO GOD

In each area of life that a Christian enters he is to raise signs to God. The clue for this is found in our Lord's words as He began His ministry. When He came to Nazareth to preach in the synagog, He said: "The Spirit of the Lord is upon Me because He hath anointed Me to preach good news to the poor. He has sent Me to proclaim release to the captives and recovering of sight to the blind, to set at liberty those who are oppressed, to proclaim the acceptable year of the Lord." As a sign of the authenticity of His own ministry, He quoted the familiar words of Isaiah 61. From His activity among the poor, the ill, the oppressed, people in His day were to recognize that God had drawn near to them. In similar fashion Christians today are to raise a sign to God's presence — His judgment and His grace — in life. We want to avoid current fads which insist that this sign will be raised only in the slum areas of inner cities by forms of the church radically different from forms we have known in the immediate past. We would insist, however, that the shape of our own ministry will approximate that of our Lord in love and compassion, in beginning with human need, in assuming the form of a servant.

It is the task of every Christian to raise this sign to God. Despite good intentions, we have failed to take seriously the reality of the church as the whole people of God. Both pastor and people refuse to believe that the church moves out into every sector of community life where a member of the body of Christ finds himself. Various proclamations of this concept may strike Christians as fresh, stimulating presentations of an idea, but they have not been strong enough to erase centuries of distinguishing between clergy and layman in such a way that only the clergyman truly represents the church. No one expects the occasional bridge player to fashion his whole life about the game as must the professional. In the real world no one expects expert knowledge and total commitment on the part of any layman as compared with the professional. The "professionalized" amateur is a predictable but rare curiosity.

This change in thinking involves more than playing with words. One can begin a tortuous avoidance of the word "layman" with no appreciable results. The fundamental picture must be changed. Try a simple experiment: Ask a group to draw a mental image of the word "church." For the vast majority the image includes a cathedral-like building. If the picture includes any human beings, there will be a clergyman, probably vested and performing a liturgical act. The falseness of the image to what we profess theologically is obvious. Here we are picturing what amounts to less than one percent of the total church, separated by a special building from any mission to the world, carrying out particular acts of worship which comprise one percent of the hours of any week.

We are, then, attempting to escape a pietistic tradition which sees the implications of the faith only within the sphere of the person and family. We are attempting to escape a dualistic tradition in which life is separated into two spheres, the sacred and the secular.

In contrast to the kraal mentality, we seek to learn what it means to live as a Christian in the world. The past emphasized the escape of the Christian from the wickedness of the world into the sanctity of the church. We seek to emphasize his conscious mission in the world. The past stressed separation; we face the necessary involvement. The past "played it safe"; we feel compelled to act, even where the situation is ambiguous. The past sought peace and the quick reconciliation of differences; we understand the dynamics of conflict and recognize it as an alternative to action where consensus is impossible. The past feared power and shied away from politics; we see the political arena as a sphere where decisions are made and therefore of great significance to the Christian.

Now while the point is made more sharply with such a rhetorical form, it oversimplifies the point and is in danger of destroying the truth. The church in seeking new forms today must not sever itself from its historic roots; we have a living continuity with the church throughout history, including history in the immediate past. In every attempt to seek a new form we run the risk of pride — we alone see the meaning of the church in the contemporary world; our models will be the prototype of the church of the 21st century. In every new form we run the risk of false judgments; the inner city and the college campuses are not the only legitimate frontiers in the late 20th century. In every new form we run the risk of apostasy; our attempt to serve may lead to an accommodation that is the latest in a long line of genuine desires to meet the world, but desires that have caused a compromise of the faith once delivered.

III. CLERGY AND LAITY

Let us investigate some implications of this view of the church manifestly present in the world through its members raising signs to God. First we highlight the necessary complementary nature of the work of clergy and laity as part of the whole people of God. Then we scan the implications of the work of the church in its gathered form. Finally we describe three areas in which God's people will raise signs to Him in the "world."

39

We need first to recover the manifold ministries within the church and to see their essential unity in Christ's reconciling ministry for the world. Manifold ministries speak to the mutual and complementary needs which clergy and laity have. Pastors are needed to proclaim and to interpret the Word of God, to administer the sacraments, to pronounce the absolution, and publicly to represent the church. In place of diminishing the pastoral office or denigrating it, this recognition frees it from many cultural expectations, from many misunderstandings. A recognition of the manifold ministries within the church will prevent the development of laicism in place of a former clericalism. A distortion in one direction is as deleterious as one in the opposite direction.

Notice what has happened in the average congregation. With no conscious attempt to direct the development in this fashion, a situation arose in which the clergyman had become the central figure. Virtually everything that happened in the congregation involved him. He was responsible. If the church became successful, he was known as a skilled organizer, builder, or preacher. If a member of his congregation shot his wife or embezzled from his employer, there arose a dark unvoiced suspicion about the true inner quality of his ministry. It was taken for granted that the interests of the congregation would reflect the pastor's personal predilections. If the man personally was interested in liturgy and youth work, the program of the parish quickly reflected his own bent over against a brother whose chief interests were preaching and the "lodge question."

The judgment has been made that this congregational pattern has made the church dependent on the minister in this last century and a half to a degree previously unknown in the history of the church. Perhaps more accurately one sees a cycle in which the church slips repeatedly into a pattern of overdependence on the clergy. Dependence certainly was not the pattern in the 300 years of church history before Constantine. Our dependence on a professional clergy would have been incomprehensible to them. During the Middle Ages the separation between the cleric and the layman became so great that the layman was relegated to a second-class position. Early reform movements and the Reformation itself attempted to correct this abuse. The father of the family was to assume the immediate spiritual care of his family. The pastor was not to assume the role of the former cleric. To the ordained was given the special ministry of Word and sacrament. To the laity was given the ministry of carrying out the task of witness and service in each calling of life where God had placed them.

But the cycle continued to move on, making the pastor the executive director of the organization of the local congregation. This affected the general direction which the interests of the congregation would assume. It also limited the amount of activity in which a local church might engage. For it was tacitly assumed by both pastor and people that he was to be in touch with every program. Since he was responsible, the pastor generally tried to keep abreast of the activities of each group by attending as many of their meetings as possible. Often unsure of his basic position in the larger society, he was reassured and flattered by this dependence of groups and individuals on him. Although they maintained the proper outward posture of humility, most pastors ruled their tiny ecclesiastical empires like kings. Because of the supposed theological expertise of their pastors, laymen assumed that this method of conducting church life was the only one possible.

The point, however, is that the total activity of the church was strictly dependent on the relationships that could be established by one man. When the man had unusual drive and ability, this activity increased. But the inherent limitation remained. (Modern studies of industry show quite clearly how many men a given person can supervise. By unconsciously assuming the model of the manager of industry, the pastor falls under all of the limitations of this pattern of operation. Further, he does so usually quite ignorant of administrative procedures which modern business takes for granted.)[3]

All of the perversion of role and the foreshortening of purpose associated with this position is the target of the new investigations of the true role of the laity. It is significant that the impetus for this movement began with the clergy. Many pastors were more unhappy with the limitations than were laymen who calmly accepted the status quo as a natural pattern of life. The goal is to reestablish a working pattern of church life in which it is apparent that all of God's people are chosen to work in the Kingdom and that His Spirit endows all of them with gifts. The Bible presents a picture of a basic equality of calling among God's people even while they have different functions. In spite of all our words about Christian callings as being of God and thus holy, we still place clergymen in a caste apart. Enough has been written about the task of the clergy to nourish, equip, and sustain the laity in their ministries in the world. We focus on the layman.

III. THE ROLE OF THE CONGREGATION

Part of the layman's task will be carried out *within the setting of the congregation.* Our indictment is that in the past this became the exclusive domain of his service. We should say that we are dealing with a calculated risk in describing this sphere of activity first. Gibbs and Morton in their stimulating book for laymen, *God's Frozen People,*[4] deliberately discuss this phase of Christian responsibility last simply because for so long it has been seen as the primary and in many cases the only domain of lay activity. That which should serve as a staging area becomes end as well as beginning. Many clergy make the serious error of feeling that the "best" laymen are those who remain close to the staging area. Three and four nights a week they are in evidence. Correction demands, however, that we see the legitimate and necessary tasks which must be performed with and for fellow believers. Having established the fact that we want to avoid "kraal keeping," what tasks are there?

First, the local church will remain the center of much of the Christian's corporate worship. Many of the splendid experiments in moving Christians out into other spheres of life have failed to see the necessity of maintaining the base at which Christians could offer their common praise and prayer and strengthen one another with the Gospel. The rhythm of gathering before scattering is necessary; the man of God must be equipped before he can carry out his role in the world. Further, he needs the concentrated moment of expressing worship to God with the fellow faithful. Indeed his whole life is to be an expression of worship. But this is usually reinforced for the one who does not exclude himself from the assembly of believers.

The recent endeavor to make the life of the organized church relate more vitally to the full life of people, individually and corporately, has arisen among those associated with liturgical revivals. For them worship is a withdrawal not *from life* but *to God*—followed by a more intense, conscious movement back into the callings of this world. They have been critical, however, of much of our worship in the immediate past, for it possesses the same weaknesses that arose from overdependence on the clergy. Worshipers have played a passive role; too often they have been spectators. This probably reached its height during the sermon, when the clergyman was the prima donna performing the role he cherished most highly. His language, his thought structures, and the quality of his theology often showed little genuine understanding of the lives of those worshiping with him.

The problem arose from a process of reducing people to a least common denominator arrived at in relationship to their degree of activity in the organized life of the church. This is the second point at which the local church will enlist people. However, church organizations will know a change of direction from that which has characterized local church life in America over the last two generations. The similarity in the organizational life of Protestant churches is remarkable. The names will vary from one denomination to another, but the basic thrust and pattern of organizations for men, women and young people are strikingly the same. Since the assembled church was falsely seen as the absolute center of the church's purpose, most of the energies of such groups were directed toward kraal keeping. One shudders as he thinks of the men of ability gathered in some churches and the low level of work presented to them.

43

This is even more striking among women. One can understand why in such large numbers they will have nothing to do with the organizational aspect of the church. Clergy have failed often to hear what they were saying. They were perhaps unconsciously piqued that they were not applauding the total program.

Such attitudes reflect dealing with them as partial people. Instead of seeing them in the richness of all of their relationships to one another and to the world, many clergy saw only their relationship to the local church. In place of seeing a man as a doctor in a position of tremendous responsibility at the local hospital—one who needed all of the aid fellow Christians could possibly give in supporting him in his crucial role—churchmen saw him as one who was "too busy" and thus poor in his attendance at church services and further as one who took no part in the organizational life of the parish. Some parishes are working hard to correct this. Some of the cell discussion groups have moved far in this direction. For in them a man consciously brings to bear all that he is in his personal and professional life.

Whether the present proliferation of small discussion groups is more than a current ecclesiastical fad that will soon run its course remains to be seen. No program or "emphasis" can be expected to maintain interest for long. Thus there are the ever weakening attempts to revitalize the interest of church people who have become jaded with all the programs we have conducted in the last decade. Potentially these discussion groups will be more than another gimmick. They are a simple structural form for permitting the people of God to carry out some of their central tasks more effectively. Ideally they focus on their purpose of bringing together the Word and life rather than on perpetuating their own organizational life. Ideally the individual group will arise to meet a purpose; it will be born, accomplish its purpose for a while, and die, to have other groups arise to carry on its purpose.

The local church can be of great assistance in leading its people to newer heights of responsible Christian living.[5] The local church should be the cross-point at which some of the critical problems facing people are discussed in the light of the Christian faith. Even though no single Christian is expected to be knowledgeable in a dozen areas of vital modern concern, a congregation should encourage different members of its fellowship to become as expert as possible in areas of interest to them. This understanding is then to be shared with fellow Christians for growth, for correction, and for decisions concerning potential answers. Such discussion must be on an adult level. This means avoiding carefully predigested topic studies that are safely removed from any arena of conflict. If such groups are merely to trace a few background facts to any contemporary issue and then discuss in the abstract possible solutions, little will be gained. Adult discussions will aim at being real. They will deal with issues that are vital; they will usually be complex issues and thus confusing and impossible of simple solution. Where possible they will result in specific individual or corporate action.

Christians will also be called to work in their local congregations in the task of educating the younger generation of believers. Churches are undergoing heart-searching in this task also. Witness the explorations and experimentation going on in Sunday schools, Christian day schools, and in organized youth work. Internal stresses will increase in such periods. The gap between national leadership and local parishes usually increases. Communication is difficult in both directions. Slogans, such as calls to relevance, may be misunderstood and at the same time may be a cover for new programs that are not offering anything very profound. It is during the early years of their lives, however, that children and young people will determine in their own minds how vital the church is to their world. If the church demonstrates that it is dealing only with peripheral items in highly dogmatic fashion, the young person, when he becomes an adult and is able to make his own decisions, will move away from the life of the church.

The local church, then, remains central as a place where people will worship, where the Word will be brought to focus on specific questions in life among fellow Christians, and where they will nurture the young in the faith.

IV. THE CHURCH IN THE WORLD

But a greater part of the Christian's life as part of the church will be lived out in the world. Our understanding of this truth is rapidly expanding these days. Consider briefly three areas in which he will raise up signs to God: in neighborhood, in work, and in leisure.

The Christian is called to participate vigorously in the life of his neighborhood as a leaven and salt. A change has come in the concept of neighborhood. This once referred to a confined geographical area in which a man lived, worked, and found his recreation. Now the neighborhood has become segmental along the lines of each function. Most men are involved with a different group of neighbors as they move from residence to work to social group to sports. Locality no longer defines all of one's neighbors. Mobility further assures a changing array of residential neighbors.

Our faith calls us to active participation within these communities of people. Gibbs and Morton admirably summarize the three lines of activity involved:

(1) Personal participation in political life, without which a democracy cannot survive;

(2) a sharing in the common corporate social activities of his neighborhood which provided the soil in which alone political democracy can grow; and

(3) personal concern in all those forms of expression — of the arts, entertainment, and propaganda — through which human values are handed on and developed and that joy expressed without which life loses any touch of glory and becomes boring.[6]

Much has been written about the more active role of Christians in political life. At this point we are not calling on people to consider politics as their career. Rather we are asking each Christian to consider his own local responsibility for corporate decisions that are made in his neighborhood and city and, on another level, for those made in his state and nation.

Such involvement necessitates a reconsideration of positions much cherished by the average Christian. Most of us do not want to become involved in areas of controversy; we want all people to think well of us. Where we are conscious of being viewed as representatives of a local church, we are further concerned that our stand will not alienate people who might be potential members. Others place the considerations of evangelism in juxtaposition to community considerations and feel that priority must be given to evangelism. Those oriented to reacting against power being exercised *over* them have great difficulty in functioning responsibly when power is given *to* them. In a democracy the latter is precisely the case. Increasingly laymen by definition of their positions will be called on to commit themselves to certain decisions; increasingly these decisions will demand "taking sides"; neutrality will simply negate any positive influence.

The relationships of a Christian on the job likewise have grown in complexity. In the past, pastors often were of marginal assistance in aiding a man to grow in his understanding of the implications of the faith on his job. While the union man in the factory was facing particular issues—usually involving conflicting communities of people who would be either aided or harmed by a decision—the pastor rarely could offer help beyond statements of the most general character. Because most of the clerical advice pertained to personal witness to Jesus Christ during free time or pointed toward a type of Christian perfectionism, most Christian men saw little opportunity for "being Christians on the job." Yet the faith speaks to many of the deeply ethical problems with which modern industry is wrestling. The relationships of the craftsman of an earlier day were much more clean-cut. Today a worker is responsible to many communities of men—some in opposition to one another. Thus a man is responsible to his employer, to his union, to his family, to the customer, to the general community, to governmental agencies exercising special controls, and to his own skills as a craftsman. The answers he needs will not come from abstract pronouncements but will begin to emerge as fellow

47

Christians—including those who know the intricacies of his work position as others know the faith in depth—wrestle together in making both immediate and long-range decisions.

How will the church strengthen its witness to its members engaged in business and industry? One answer has developed in the Detroit Industrial Mission.[7] Bishop Richard Emrich of the Episcopal Diocese of Michigan was one of the key founders of the DIM. He saw the need clearly: "We have in America an industrial society dominated by giant corporations. Yet the church has no relevance to the great industrial society." The result, he said, is that "the tremendous insights of our spiritual heritage are not applied to industry." In order to rewin the world of work as a specific area of Christian concern, DIM was begun some 8 years ago. The staff meets with men in approximately two dozen industry-related endeavors in Detroit. Its parish includes the production line as well as the executive suites. The task is not to convert or to argue the merits of a church. The task is to highlight the moral dimensions of the decisions which men are making. The hourly rate workers meeting during lunch breaks talk over union elections, job security, and the implications of politics. White collar employees discuss such items as costs, employee relations, and promotion policies. Managers tend to deal with subjects even broader in scope, studying the relationship of their industry to the broader society. The clergy members of the staff are there to prod and provoke and to serve as theological resource. They seek to bring the men to take a position on the political and economic issues they face. That the DIM has begun to meet a need is evidenced by the fact that similar missions are developing in other major metropolitan areas across the country.

The Christian in America will find himself dealing increasingly with the area of leisure. Some have felt it indicative of the church's usual pace of relevance that it has "discovered" the world of industry at the very moment when automation will release larger numbers of people from prolonged hours in factories. All—whether through unemployment or through reduced working hours and lengthened vacations—will know

48

an increased amount of leisure time. In his outstanding study, *Of Time, Work and Leisure,*[8] Sebastian de Grazia reminds the modern reader of the ancient's view of leisure—in Aristotle's words, the state of "freedom from the necessity of labor." For the ancient world leisure was primary; work was that which took one away. Post-Reformation thinking recovered the values inherent in work. But in recovering the meaning of work the values of leisure were slighted. Perhaps a false puritanism causes moderns still to feel a bit guilty when they are not at work. Primarily the confusion for most Americans is to equate "free time"—time not spent in gaining the necessities of life—with leisure. Free time opens the opportunity for leisure; it does not automatically produce it. The church is crucially placed to deal with this challenge: it affects people; it deals with the question of values; the church has been involved in creating the present set of values and attitudes; the church already is dealing with people during their free time; the church has the unique opportunity of linking people with free time to situations for intellectual growth and genuine service.

In this chapter we have attempted to avoid thinking of the church as a protective kraal. The task of the Christian is to raise signs to God wherever he goes. Part of this work will be carried on within the local congregation. There the worship and prayers of the group will center, the common celebration of the sacraments, the education of all within the fellowship, particularly the young. It will provide the matrix within which the Word can be brought to bear on specific situations of need. Much more, however, will go on within the given structures and natural settings of the community. In particular the areas of neighborhood, work, and leisure present some of the greatest immediate challenges. Thorwald Bender reminded us that we always stand in an inescapable relationship to God and to our fellowmen. "Man stands *ontologically* inseparable from God," he writes, "and *ethically* inseparable from mankind." We are part of the church that lives between the times— between God and man, between Creation and Judgment.

NOTES FOR CHAPTER 3

[1] Klaus von Bismarck, "The Laity: The Church in the World," *Laity,* No. 13 (February 1962), p. 5.

[2] *The Epistle to Diognetus: The Greek Text with Introduction,* trans. and notes by Henry G. Meecham (Manchester University Press, 1949), pp. 78 – 79.

[3] In industry a skilled manager is able to supervise seven people effectively. An individual can have some degree of personal relationship with an upper limit of only 200 persons.

[4] Mark Gibbs and Thomas R. Morton, *God's Frozen People: A Book for and About Christian Laymen* (Philadelphia: Westminster Press, 1965).

[5] For a critical response to those emphasizing a secular gospel and rejecting the possibility of parish renewal, see Landon Gilkey, *How the Church Can Minister to the World Without Losing Itself* (New York: Harper & Row, 1964).

[6] Gibbs and Morton, p. 94.

[7] Copies of their reports, "Occasional Papers in Christian Faith and Industrial Society," may be obtained from the Rev. Robert C. Batchelder, Detroit Industrial Mission, 7109 West McNichols, Detroit, Mich. 48221.

[8] Sebastian de Grazia, *Of Time, Work and Leisure* (New York: Twentieth Century Fund, 1962).

50

4

Emerging Shapes of the Church's Life

THEORETICAL CONSIDERATIONS

Forms of church life is one of the major questions faced by Western Christendom within the last decade. Volumes of merciless criticism have appeared concerning inherited forms of the church which are proving to be increasingly ineffective as instruments for reaching many problems of the 20th century. Protestant churches in radically different sociological settings have committed themselves to various types of experimental ministries as exploratory attempts to find forms that might prove more useful. As the years stretch out and discussions and pilot projects continue, some people are growing restive as they see relatively little impact on the organized life of the church. Elite groups in the church are aware of these efforts and their significance; yet the great stream of church life flows on as if the efforts had never taken place.

In this chapter we propose to investigate some of the key thinking that lies behind some of the attempts at renewal.[1] In the next chapter we survey the major directions which this experimentation has taken, describing some of the most significant endeavors.

One discovers a mixed reaction to the preoccupation with new forms both on the level of theologians and administrators and among "church folk." Hoekendijk warned early in

51

the period of renewal—in 1952—that preoccupation with ecclesiology is a sign of decadence. Instead of being concerned with the spread of the Gospel and the relevance of the faith to the lives of people, this appears to be an introverted preoccupation with oneself. Concern with questions of the church displaces questions that should occupy the life of theologian, pastor, and people. Standing at the opposite end are the statements prepared for the first report on the main theme at the meeting of the World Council of Churches at Evanston in 1954: "Without radical changes of structure and organization, our existing churches will never become missionary churches, which they must if the gospel is to be heard in the world."[2]

In the intervening years many individual church bodies set a priority on the question of form and structure—not, however, to evade the question of mission but precisely as *an instrument to* mission.

In our approach to this material we adopt a sympathetic yet critical stance. Occasionally it seems that one is expected either to applaud each new venture conjured up by any clergyman anywhere in the Western world or to exert all of his energies toward preserving the status quo. We proceed, then, by exploring four basic statements descriptive of these attempts to discover shapes of the church that will be more useful for mission.

1. *New forms of the church continue to emerge.* In referring to the inevitability of this process, Marty reminds us that in order to keep a post white, you must keep painting it white or it naturally turns grey and eventually black.[3] Similarly one must actively work to preserve the status quo; otherwise one has inevitable change. The form may be thought of as being the same as in the past—consider the residential parish within the last century and a half—but to meet changed situations, it undergoes many profound changes. Sociologically the parts of a culture must continually be brought into balance. No institution that is out of balance can long survive. Thus the residential parish has made many adjustments to its surrounding culture in the last 150 years. The contemporary critics are

asking whether its changes have been such that its usefulness is sharply curtailed for serving other needs which have arisen during this same period.

New forms have arisen in the past to meet specialized needs. We have the development of chaplaincies to the military, to hospitals and nursing homes, to the university community, to areas of homeless men, etc. But these are viewed as subsidiaries to the residential ministry. Those supervising these specialized areas were aware of the high rate of attrition as their men one by one felt the strong pull back into "the regular ministry." But now the "morphological fundamentalists" are on the defensive, attempting to defend a form that is charged with being irrelevant to the major challenges of our modern day.

Perhaps too much of the recent discussion on forms has taken place in the tense atmosphere of charge and countercharge. When this occurs, the more important questions regarding the purpose and task of the church are submerged. The question of *form* must follow that of function. Any form of the church is provisional, including the residential parish. It is useful only as long as it is the most useful shape for the people of God to assume in carrying out their primary tasks in the world. In many cases the parish form has served as a deterrent preventing people from responding as church within the structures in the world of which they are a part.

A growing number of perceptive people are becoming disillusioned with the rigidity and inflexibility of forms of the church which have been seen as normative in the recent past. Life within such churches has begun to seem hollow. A pastor who has worked for new forms to serve the world described the fellowship of the average congregation as a "colorless insipidity." There is nothing distinctive about its fellowship; there is nothing in the values and behavior of its people that could not be found in the local service club. The religion evidenced by its members is a dependent variable—it does not initiate new modes of life and conduct; it imitates what it sees about it. Like other organizations, churches appear to be primarily interested in institutional success—number of members, image in the community, size and quality of plant, and increase in budget.

While some are making dramatic ventures into various new channels of ministry, others quietly suggest that God's Spirit will lead us to find the new forms. Rather than *seek* new forms, they would interpret them as a thing *received* from God. God is the Giver of the new wine*skin* as well as the new wine. Robert Raines writes: "It is not by our ingenuity that the reformation comes but by our obedient perception and reception of the new shapes God is preparing. There is, then, a paradoxical urgency and nonchalance about our waiting upon the Lord." [4]

2. *The residential parish can no longer serve as the only normative structure of the Western church, but it can remain a viable form for some time.* Militants on both sides of the question will quarrel with this statement. The structural fundamentalists insist on the parish as a God-given form that will never disappear. Critics of the residential parish are so sweeping in their indictments of it that they see no hope of renewal within that form.

If asked, the average member of a congregation would see a strong fundamental similarity in ecclesiastical structure between the form of church life of the New Testament period and that of his own day. The modern parish of course is of relatively recent vintage. Less than 200 years old, it is a product of the industrial revolution. Although the term "parish" tempts us to seek its beginning in the medieval parish concept, the congregation as we know it arose and developed in response to the new mobility of people that occurred as a result of the industrial revolution. The old feudal type of territorialism was doomed with the uprooting of people and their movement to city or town where their skills or their hands were in demand. The new free voluntary gathering of peoples into congregations was ideally suited to meet the new need.

Within the two decades since World War II, however, a series of changes have occurred which make impossible demands of the congregation. And the congregation is proving too inflexible to meet the new demands. It is charged with being irrelevant. So sympathetic a man as Elton Trueblood judges: "It is hard to exaggerate the degree to which the modern church seems irrelevant to modern man."[5]

The man on the street needs no sociologist to document the fact that the simple homogeneous community of the past, where a man lived all facets of life, has been shattered. Riesman has shown that modern man receives his impulses not from those geographically proximate but from new centers of authority.[6] The modern young person is attuned more sensitively to moral codes, values, and fashions emanating from Hollywood or New York than he is to those propounded in the local church basement by a middle-aged Sunday school teacher. The parish is weakest in dealing with the new society with its new authorities, its mass media approaches, and with the whole arena of life described as the "public sphere."[7] The parish seems to be tied to the private sphere. It can baptize a child, but it seems powerless to lead the baptized adult into being the church at the center of politics or of business and industry. It can solemnize marriages as an agent of the state but fails to affect the values that dominate our culture in the areas of sex morality and family life. It stands by to offer personal consolation but remains a weak second in the public mind to the psychiatrist. It gathers its little knots of faithful members into its organizations, but the organizations remain without practical influence in the life of even the local community.

The parish has become an institution that absorbs so many of the energies of its members for the perpetuation and enlargement of itself that it is ill suited to a servant ministry in a world of need. Decisions regarding any action are unconsciously weighed in the light of what they will do for the church itself. By definition it can take no part in unpopular causes; it cannot be involved where there is a difference of opinion; it cannot be involved for long in programs which will not produce their own revenue. Thus the local church finds itself unable to generate values and to lead people to see how

55

the faith might express itself in the marketplace. It rests content with the crumbs—the invitation to the clergyman on ceremonial occasions when no decisions are to be made, or to membership on boards which are channels for eliciting community support for programs planned safely apart from churchly influences. To a shocking degree our churches have contented themselves with pronouncing a benediction on the status quo.

If the parish is institutionally geared primarily to its own preservation, removed from the mainstream of public life, static in a day of vast change, irrelevant to the most pressing questions of our day, related to a specific territory while life has become increasingly dialogical, is there any chance of rescuing the congregation and shaping it again into an effective instrument for the service of God? The most militant critics—for instance, Berger and Winter—answer with a decisive "No!"[8] For some time we have been getting feedback from various agencies of government, expressing the thought that church life as we presently know it is doomed to extinction within the next 10 years.

There are others of us who are less pessimistic about the present parish. Most would agree with the major part of the diagnosis. The problems of dislocation are serious. Still we see the possibility of renewal within the parish. Among the men whom we have mentioned, Marty and Raines stand as articulate spokesmen for renewal of the parish rather than its necessary death before relevance can be achieved. The bones are becoming dry, but God still can breathe life into these dead bones. The cultural rubbish may be blocking much life within parishes, but Word and sacrament remain as life-instilling sources. The parish may serve for a relatively brief moment in the total history of the church, but its day does not yet appear to be ended.

In the previous chapter we viewed some of the tasks which the local church could uniquely assume. Behind these assumptions was the strong insistence that the individual Christian needs the support and correction of the corporate group whenever possible. We take the church seriously. This

56

implies some corporate structuring of Christians who are thus brought together. God calls us not to solitary sainthood but to fellowship in a company of committed men. In contrast to frequently quoted Eastern statements to the contrary, we are called not to light isolated candles in the darkness but to be part of a focused light which God Himself generates. This involves changing some strongly held views of contemporary church members. Most people who join a church fail to appreciate the corporate nature of the church. They see themselves basically as "consumers" of religion, of which the clergyman is the chief purveyor. Thus in a fashion not too dissimilar from the way they select detergents or TV programs, they select their church. While outward friendliness is a treasured folkway in local churches, this is rarely understood or appreciated as extending to honest care of another. The body of Christ is a Biblical expression to be expected in liturgy and sermon, but any attempt to spell out its serious implications in contemporary terms is quietly discounted as a lovely but impossible ideal.

Even those who would plead most eloquently for the continuation of the parish would be forced to admit that the conventional structures within churches are not geared to bringing people into deep personal relationships with one another. Yet this is precisely what is needed if the local church is to accomplish its task. On the local level the parish is to knit individuals together into a webbing of people that will strengthen the person and provide an immediate channel for his ministry. The pilgrimage is to be shared. Witness, whenever possible, is to be strengthened by becoming a corporate witness. The individual Christian standing alone in factory, office, slum, or college dormitory is measurably strengthened when he is consciously there as part of the church — and when the church in tangible fashion supports his endeavor.

Each church probably will assume a slightly different shape if its structure is truly appropriate to its particular mission. Each Christian will find his life being subtly reshaped as he finds his place in a small family of God in a local place. The colorless uniformity that comes from seeing each person only in a highly segmental fashion will fade as each is brought into the fellowship to share the strengths he has as gifts which God has provided. Ephesians 4 still suggests the model for our day. God still provides the gifts which His church needs, and He provides the situations in which the church will be able to carry out its task.

We are not ready to abandon the local congregation because of our clever plans for forms to supplant it. We are interested in having the church do the work God gives to it. This demands having the church trained and deployed as an army in enemy territory. We are seeking a strategy which will best accomplish this. In this period of experimentation we are proceeding with a pattern of trial and error, meanwhile retaining continuity with the parish pattern of the past century and a half.

3. *The emerging shapes are concerned primarily with having the church again face the world as servant.* In the more stable world of our immediate agricultural past it was easy to concentrate on the church as a gathered community which would send a few missionaries out into segments of the pagan world. Our understanding of the church, of its mission, and of the world has deepened. The awareness broke in upon us that our task as church was not to make forays out into the world to snatch a person or two to join us in the fortress. Rather we were an army that was to spend the major part of its time "out there." Even that picture breaks down as we become a church genuinely oriented to the world. For we quickly discover that the oversimplified judgments made while we were safely entrenched behind the fortress were inadequate when we were in the world. We are sent to participate in Christ's basic mission to the world. This involved, He said, saving the world, not judging it.

We have difficulty in operating on the basis of this view. True, in conferences and in sermons we have been told to think of ourselves as a "sent" people. The words "apostolic" and "mission" have been applied to the whole church. Disciples are glimpsed for a moment as the salt and light of the world, as leaven in the lump, as sheep sent into the midst of wolves. But our structures prevented us from making any fundamental change from being sheep safely corralled in a pasture. It is easy to exaggerate the necessity of the function of either the gathered or the scattered church. But it is most fruitful to see that the two must be kept in tension. Hendrik Kraemer once said that every Christian needs two conversions: first to Christ and then to the world.[9]

Some of the most creative renewal of the church has taken place where the church engaged the world in an attempt to transform the world. Joseph H. Oldham has reminded us that it is false to think of the church as a separate sphere of existing reality.[10] It is not a kingdom that occupies a given place. It is not distinct from the natural world and its history. Rather it is a new dimension of reality penetrating these realms and transforming them. The concept of a separate religious sphere is shattered. The work of the church is to find its center and its reality in everyday life. This means that the church must enter into the whole of the structure of society. No structure is so corrupt that it places itself beyond the reach of God's healing as it is conveyed through the message and service of the church.

This is at the heart of the church's mission. For God sent the church into the world to be His agent of renewal. The church denies its very existence when it becomes a closed corporation devoted simply to self-perpetuation. For the church received its mission from the God who creates, redeems, and makes alive. Christ described the pattern: "As the Father has sent Me, even so I send you." Thus He sends His church into every realm of the world as He was sent to the world by the Father.

In these days many church bodies are reminding themselves of the tremendous scope of this task: that the church is Christ's mission to the whole man, to the whole church, to the whole society, to the whole world.

The church is Christ's mission to the whole man.[11] For man must be viewed in his totality. We are not concerned with some part of man designated as his "soul." Even as man is

59

physical and spiritual, so our concern for him is both physical and spiritual. A theological view of man which restricts itself to dealing with a mere spiritual being is as extreme and incomplete as one that views man as a mere physical being. The Bible has an earthiness that seems to embarrass some moderns. For it makes clear that God is concerned with all of man — that God created and loves his body as much as his mind or soul. It follows, then, that how a man lives, where he lives, how he earns his living, whether he receives adequate medical treatment, where his children play and go to school, the quality of their teachers, the way he is treated as a citizen and human being — these are all a vital part of the church's concern about the "whole man."

For the church must reflect the concern of her Lord, who pointedly addressed Himself to the physical, social, economic, and political concerns of men. Jesus healed the sick, fed the hungry, condemned the artificial criteria by which social outcasts were produced, spoke of exploitation, of obsession with the material, and clarified the place and role of government. In each of these actions Christ was asserting His Lordship over the entire world.

The church moreover, claims to be Christ's mission to the whole of society.[12] By this the church acknowledges that God intends social structures for the well-being of man. But man can and does use these structures demonically for his own ends. Because of God's fundamental concern, however, the church is commissioned with a corporate responsibility toward the structures of society. Its task is to witness to God's purpose for the institutions of life and to witness against every human perversion in society that frustrates God's intention for man.

The Christian is given the task of being this agent of reconciliation as he confronts needs in family life, on the job, within the local community, and finally in the larger community of nation and world. The church is called to responsible participation in the world at its points of deepest need. We are all wrestling with the problem of deployment. How can we most

60

effectively bring this witness and service? No simple formula will work in every setting, yet the proposal to go with a heart of genuine service stained by no ulterior motive is clear. The pattern of the Servant seen in our Lord provides the best model for His followers.

Some Christians who have in the past worked with a clear distinction between "spiritual" work (dealing with souls) and secondary tasks of "secular" work (dealing with minds and bodies) fear the loss of the church's clear witness. They fear involvement in areas of need where many other people — many outspokenly non-Christian — are involved. But the Christian cannot wait for the world to become more tidy. He must work in the midst of the world as it is constituted. Yet there frequently will be a difference between the service performed by a Christian and that performed by one who does not know Christ. The one involved sees it in a dozen small ways. His interpretation of the situation, his basic motivation, his resources will be strikingly different at a number of points from those of his counterpart in the world. When the fellow worker begins to sense this difference, he raises the question of faith. The role of genuine servant is so rare today that when the world sees it in an authentic form, it creates a situation for witness by raising the question of the source of goal and motivation.

Those who spend their lives in such ministry share a number of convictions. The ministry of service is born within Christian fellowship. An individual may respond to a particular need. Usually he has been awakened and sustained by Christian community. Discipleship precedes apostleship. One must be patient in attempting to bring another to a sense of ministering service. When one sees responsive action as the natural and inevitable result of faith, he may become impatient with those in whom this awareness is slow in developing. The history of the church in the last decade demonstrates the need for love and patience in interpreting this as a vital and intrinsic part of the life of the church.

Furthermore, this service must reach out to those in greatest need. Historically the diaconic ministry of the church

61

reached out to "the least" in caring for the sick, the feeble, the mentally ill, the orphans, the aged, and the prisoners. In society as a whole such people are pushed to the fringes as insignificant or even useless; they form a burden which only the Christian will assume with joy. Finally this work as a servant people in our day will be as ecumenical as possible; it will frequently demand new and unconventional forms. The world has been surprised when it found unity and love among those from different church bodies among whom it expected suspicion and parochialism. The world has been astounded to find imagination and vigor within the church when it expected only dullness and preservation of the status quo.

The final marks of the newer forms which impress one involve the flexible and expendable quality of the work. The men involved in these ministries have tried to learn from history and do not institutionalize the newer forms in such a way that long after they have outlived their usefulness they are destined to continue their operation. Change is so rapid that many forms will serve for only a brief period before major adjustments must be made or another approach utilized. Though the church has always possessed a theology that emphasized the necessity for being ready to give its own life in service, practical church life took the other route of utilizing its energies first for the preservation of the institution. In our day men are seeking forms which will be truly expendable, forms that can die when they have performed the service for which they were devised. This is the ultimate test of servanthood.

4. *In fashioning new shapes the church must make sure that it remains church with the message of justification close to its heart and the Gospel as its motivation.* No problem regarding the new shapes of the church is more troublesome; ultimately none is more crucial. As the church has reemphasized its servant role and as it has come to see God at work in the secular spheres of life, the question of the form which its own involvement should take has become extremely difficult. As long as the dichotomy of body and soul, church and world could be maintained, the sphere of the church's operation was clear.

Now that the whole world enters the area of the church's concern and ministry, the form of the church's involvement becomes a major question.[13]

We possess a strong tradition regarding definition of the church and an understanding of its role in the world. The definition centers in Article VII of the Augsburg Confession: "The Church is the congregation of saints, in which the Gospel is rightly taught and the Sacraments are rightly administered." Over the years we have attempted to preserve the dynamic quality of this insight and to refuse to permit it to become static. Thus the church is seen as continually formed by the Gospel and not the Law. The church is the *ekklesia,* those whom God is calling out of the world through faith in Jesus Christ. It is the community of those who are *simul justi et peccatores,* a community of sinners who daily receive the forgiving Word. Our traditional stance perhaps has not been as strong in emphasizing that the quality of being called out of the world does not mean withdrawal from the world in its needs. Though we have avoided the dangers of pietism, we have developed a form of church life which has withdrawn from the centers of community life. The church has had little to do with the marketplace of the political arena. The world became an arena from which people were snatched to the safety of the church.

One of the strongest voices raised against the resulting quietism was that of Bonhoeffer and his concept of cheap grace:

> Cheap grace is the preaching of forgiveness without requiring repentance, baptism without Church discipline, Communion without confession, absolution without contrition. Cheap grace is grace without discipleship, grace without the Cross, grace without Jesus Christ, living and incarnate.[14]

Many found that Bonhoeffer struck a responsive chord in their thinking. This group was not abandoning the Gospel for a new law. It involves grace, but it is costly precisely because of what it meant to our Lord: "Such grace is *costly* because it calls us to follow, and it is *grace* because it calls us to follow *Jesus Christ.* It is costly because it costs a man

63

his life and it is grace because it gives a man the only true life. It is costly because it condemns sin, and grace because it justifies the sinner. Above all, it is *costly* because it cost God the life of His Son. . . ."[15]

The church with an awareness of "costly grace" works with a sense of integrity. It makes clear that it is calling people to a life of discipleship. It does not enlist people with false appeals to their sense of comfort or their desire for happiness. It does not proceed on the basis of community expectation. This insight broke in upon a sensitive Christian who moved from the state of being a passive church member to an "active" one. In reflecting on the evangelism program of his church, he said it bore a striking resemblance to his approach to new golfers in the neighborhood: ". . . we spoke eloquently about our fine senior minister (the golf pro) and his skill and allure — about our elaborate physical plant (the clubhouse) and its facilities — about our fine membership (social rank and status) — but little or nothing about the opportunity for fellowship in Christ."

The church that is aware of "costly grace" moves out into the structures of the world to serve and to transform, but it does so with an awareness of its unique contribution. We have already referred to its self-giving service. In this it reflects the love that our Lord has for each creature. It seeks out conditions and levels of need not met by others and offers itself in personal service. But because it *is not* sentimental and *is* serious about meeting needs — and not just performing good works — it attempts to work with the underlying condition, not simply the symptom. This forces it to deal with the structures of society as well as the individual. For today the structures form molds which determine many aspects of personal life.

In all of this, however, the church is aware of its unique role. On the one hand the church is released from any illusions about building an empire. Ideally the church attempts to serve and not thereby to gain any advantage. On the other hand, while it will find itself working with many people and organiza-

64

tions with totally alien allegiances and motivations, it nevertheless serves also in these domains. Within a given case of racial conflict, some may be there because of Marxist convictions, others to attempt to gain leadership and power; others may be fighting for the future welfare of their children; and others may find it most expedient because of their position vis-à-vis the Negro community. But the churchman is there because he has been sent by Jesus Christ. His motivation, his goals, and his resources are different. He is motivated by the Gospel. His goal is to offer to the others all the gifts that God has made available — minimally justice in the social sphere, ideally the gift of life in Jesus Christ. His resources include more than his own intense concern; he comes in the power of our Lord. In the midst of a situation that appears utterly hopeless he possesses the hope which God has brought in His Son.

Since the Fourth Assembly of the Lutheran World Federation at Helsinki, in 1963, the Lutheran Church has been struggling with the question of how to speak the message of justification most meaningfully to modern man. Some of the subsequent discussion is helpful to us. For it has been reaffirmed once again that justification creates fellowship. The message of the Gospel is truncated if it is limited to its meaning to the individual. Justification means that the church is not a fellowship of righteous persons but a fellowship of pardoned sinners who in obedience go back into the world to serve. A discussion group in Hungary suggests the need for a self-revision of Lutheranism on the basis of its own doctrine of justification:

> It must come out of its cool reserve, take upon itself fellowship with the world of today, for Jesus Christ's sake, and share in the solution of the great question of the contemporary world . . . it is also true that Lutheranism rightly proclaims and represents the Gospel of world-embracing love only when it gives itself in the same love for service to the world of today.[16]

65

[1] Cf. *Dialog,* IV (Winter 1965). The whole issue is devoted to "New Forms for the Church."

[2] Cf. *Union Seminary Quarterly Review,* X, 1 (November 1954), for a number of articles evaluating the Evanston Assembly, especially Searle M. Bates, "Evangelism and Missions at Evanston," pp. 21 – 26.

[3] Cf. Martin E. Marty: *The New Shape of American Religion* (New York; Harper & Brothers, 1959); *Second Chance for American Protestants* (New York: Harper & Row, 1963); Kyle Haselden and Martin Marty, eds., *What's Ahead for the Churches?* (New York: Sheed and Ward, 1964).

[4] Robert Raines, *Reshaping the Christian Life* (New York: Harper & Row, 1964), p. 8.

[5] Cf. David Elton Trueblood, *The Company of the Committed* (New York: Harper & Brothers, 1961).

[6] David Riesman, Nathan Glazer, and Revel Denny, *The Lonely Crowd* (New Haven: Yale University Press, 1950); David Riesman, *Individualism Reconsidered and Other Essays* (Glencoe, Ill.: Free Press, 1954).

[7] Cf. "Christians in Power Structures," theme of the WCC Bulletin, *Laity,* No. 14 (November 1962).

[8] Peter L. Berger, *The Precarious Vision* (New York: Doubleday & Co., 1963); Gibson Winter, *The New Creation as Metropolis* (New York: The Macmillan Co., 1963).

[9] Hendrik Kraemer, *A Theology of the Laity* (Philadelphia: The Westminster Press, 1959).

[10] Joseph H. Oldham, *Life Is Commitment* (New York: Harper & Row, 1953).

[11] In its 46th convention The Lutheran Church – Missouri Synod passed a series of mission affirmations that described the church's mission to the whole man. The Last Judgment will be a report of whether or not we fed, clothed, and visited our Lord in the least of His hungry, naked, and forsaken brethren.

> Therefore Christians, individually and corporately, prayerfully seek to serve the needs of the total man. Christians bring the Good News of the living Christ to dying men. They bring men instruction in all useful knowledge. They help and befriend their neighbor on our small planet in every bodily need. They help their neighbor to improve and protect his property and business by bringing him economic help and enabling him to earn his daily bread in dignity and self-respect. Christians minister to the needs of the whole man, not because they have forgotten the witness of the Gospel but because they remember it. They know that the demonstration of their faith in Christ adds power to its demonstration. [*Proceedings of the Forty-sixth Regular Convention of The Lutheran Church – Missouri Synod,* June 16 – 26, 1965, Resolution 1-01 E, p. 81]

[12] In suggesting that the Christian recognizes no separate area of life that may be termed "secular," the convention described the difficulties one faces in determining the shape of corporate actions:

> That Christians be encouraged to seek the peace of the city, as God commands, working together with their fellow

citizens of the nation and of the world, whatever their race, class, or belief . . .

That Christians be encouraged as they attempt, under the judgment and forgiveness of God, to discover and further His good purposes in every area of life, to extend justice, social acceptance, and a full share in God's bounty to all people who are discriminated against and oppressed by reason of race, class, creed, or other unwarranted distinctions. [Ibid., Resolution 1-01 D, p. 81]

[13] For a Lutheran theological critique of much current involvement see George W. Forell, "Lutherans in the Ecumenical Movement," *Lutheran World*, XII, 3 (1965), 257-63.

[14] Dietrich Bonhoeffer, *The Cost of Discipleship* (London: SCM Press, 1937; rev. ed., 1959).

[15] Ibid., p. 37.

[16] *Justification Today: Studies and Reports*. Published and edited by the Commission and Department of Theology. Supplement to *Lutheran World*, No. 1 (1965), p. 60

5

Emerging Shapes of the Church's Life

ILLUSTRATIONS OF RENEWAL

My contacts as Director of Urban Seminars for 2 years have disclosed some 30 individual efforts — approaches, pilot programs, creative insights — that might be shared. Rather than divide these new shapes arbitrarily into parish, interparish, and broader-community units, we shall envision a continuum that moves from programs of the gathered church on the local level to considerations that affect the church nationally. By placing the noteworthy projects into nine larger categories, we hope the accent will fall on the *implications* of these new shapes for our churches. In most cases one finds several groups following similar patterns; therefore we examine the shape without undue consideration of the individuals and specific churches involved.

1. Rich Programs of Community Service Provided by Inner-City Churches for Their Communities. In New York, Chicago, Detroit, San Francisco, San Antonio we find old congregations situated in areas of intense human need. Most of these churches are in areas where newcomers to the city first settle. Most of these come with few skills. They move into a city that seems alien and hostile. Problems of personal and familial adjustment are great. Here people are confronted with stark poverty, spiritual hunger, family disorganization, bad housing, illegitimacy, brutality, and mayhem. They do not experience these raw realities in the bloodless, detached, and objective way that we do. To meet these deep human problems, the churches offer many community services: medical and dental clinics, educational programs for the preschool kindergarten children to prepare them for formal schooling, homemaking classes for women who lack the basic skills in caring for a family, athletics and recreational programs for young people, creative arts programs for various ages, clubs and councils which support community service projects and address special interests.

The low-income population has a myriad of needs. Obviously one of the most important is the economic need. Most of these people must develop an "economic literacy," the ability to understand the practical workings of our modern economic society and how to get ahead in it. As a tool some churches have established credit unions, where people can aid one another financially, where they are able to learn the ABCs of economy and savings.

Inner-city congregations also are attempting to meet the needs of people where family support is minimal. The church goes out of its way to accept neighborhood children, whether or not their parents come to church. By providing professional and volunteer workers to spend time with them, the church provides a substitute for the father, who in the majority of cases in given housing areas is absent. In an attempt to meet some of the intellectual, emotional, and social needs of slum children, the church has been forced to define its own role more sharply. What role is the church to play in those cases that transcend social service? In view of its total task, what priority should the church give to such needs? What is the relationship of the church to the schools, the public and private welfare agencies within the community?

2. Variations on the Parish Model. Recognizing the strengths of the parish as we have known it in the immediate past, some have been seeking forms in which these strengths might be maintained and some of the most glaring weaknesses of the contemporary urban parish might at the same time be

70

eliminated. One weakness results from the homogeneity of interest that develops from the natural restrictions imposed by the residential pattern. Parochialism develops because parishioners are not confronted by those who are different from them. They do not serve, because so much of the need is hidden from them. They are not forced to hear political and economic views at variance with their own, because of the relative homogeneity of education, income, and professional responsibility within a given community.

There has been some experimentation with the "metropolitan parish." This is a congregation of families drawn together on the basis of one or two families from each congregation within the total metropolitan community. They join the metropolitan parish for a stipulated period, say 2 years. Pastoral service is provided by the diocese or district. The group avoids owning real estate by meeting in buildings which churches and their agencies already own. The focus is on developing a "lay elite" to carry out whatever specific mission may lie at hand. No special financing has been necessary in that the usual pledges of the members are directed to the work of the metropolitan parish. The group emphasizes special training. At the end of the stipulated period the families return to their home congregations.

Another suggestion for modifying the existing parish structure involves the deliberate mixing of class and racial lines by establishing a "sector parish." Instead of the church serving a residential area in a general circle about the church building, people are recruited along a long, thin line — perhaps along a major expressway or rapid-transit line. Thus people representing various segments of society — educationally, economically, professionally, and ethnically diverse — are drawn together in one parish. A firsthand acquaintance with needs and an availability of resources are brought together in a fruitful fashion.

The conventional parish structure was challenged by the emergence of great high-rise complexes of middle-class or luxury apartments, such as Marina City, Chicago. The pilot

71

program set three goals for itself: (1) to serve as a listening post for the churches; (2) to witness to Jesus Christ and His meaning to life; (3) to train Christians to serve as the church in that place. To implement these goals the pastor conducted conversations and conferences with those who were able to reflect on the meaning of this new form of community life. He formed a training class to include all Christians. An art group was formed to test the use of special-interest groups. In speaking of the visible shape of Christianity in the high-rise, the pastor reflected the residents' determination not to become involved with the church as institution. Most had had enough contact with the local church as manifested in a building that they wanted no part in any program that would take that route. A simple cell-group approach seemed preferable as a means of bringing together Christians and those in the world whom they should meet.

Many of the new forms question a basic facet of the present parish structure: its parochialism. In at least a half dozen cities attempts are being made to have churches realize their mutual responsibility and interdependence. Aware of the dangers of parochial isolationism and selfishness, groups of established congregations and missions are forming various structures directed toward making a reality of their common responsibility for the work of the church in their cities. This always has manifested itself to a degree within a given denomination, but the challenge here is to investigate points at which several denominations can work cooperatively. We have gone far in the last decade in reducing the envy and sense of competition which often served as strong motivation behind denominational programs. In most cities the problems have become so large and so complex that unilateral decisions are no longer responsible. Some of the values demonstrated in team ministries find expression on a higher level in this type of coordinated planning.

3. New Shapes in Christian Education. Among the vast changes taking place in this arena we shall focus on only three items as illustrations of the type of thinking and experimenting afoot. First, a growing number of congregations have begun an attempt to upgrade the discipline and Christian understanding of its membership. One model, followed by others, instituted a School for Christian Living. Prior to membership in the church a person is expected to take six courses; refresher courses are taken subsequently by those already in membership. Required courses are presented in Old and New Testament, Doctrine, Christian Growth, Ethics, and Stewardship. After a year's exposure in the school, those who feel called by our Lord into the fellowship of His church write a brief paper telling what Christ means to them, a statement of what spiritual disciplines they currently are following, a statement regarding the areas of life in which they still need help, and a statement on the tasks they are currently engaged in for the church and on other work to which they may feel called. Obviously such an approach has produced fewer members, but they possess a new degree of understanding and commitment.

Congregations in inner-city situations faced extreme frustrations in attempting to use denominationally produced educational material that obviously was addressed to middle-class children and youth. Further, many suburban congregations searched for good educational materials that would interpret their role of responsibility in being interdependent Christians in the modern metropolis. The last 5 years have seen vigorous experimentation in the production of materials to meet these needs. The interdenominational mission education theme for 1963 − 64 was "The Changing City Challenges the Church." Every major denomination brought out an array of materials to interpret this theme to virtually every age group in the church. This went far toward meeting the second need. Meanwhile many local congregations began to produce their own materials for use with slum children. After some refinements, part of this material is now available through denominational publishers.

A final category of need focuses on the church's attempt to aid children who are unprepared for school programs as presently constituted. Recent programs have emphasized that slum children begin school seriously behind other children on the first day. Educationally, socially, and emotionally these youngsters are unprepared for formal education. By first grade they are behind other children whose homes have provided a rich source of experience that enables them to be mentally alert, to deal with abstractions, and to have a healthy curiosity about their experiences. By third grade they are potential dropouts. Churches have attacked this challenge at two points. By starting with children at the age of 3 and 4, churches and other agencies have attempted to enrich the culturally starved environment of these preschool children. These programs, to be effective, have been extended to deal with the child from age 3 through the third grade. For the children already past these ages tutorial programs or courses in remedial reading have been instituted.

A sizable number of churches have made significant contributions to children in their neighborhoods through the introduction of remedial reading programs. Many youngsters in slum schools have great difficulty in learning to read at their grade level because of poor home conditions, because English may not be their native language, and because of the lower quality of their schools. With limited funds a church can set up such a service program with a part-time consultant and some committed volunteer workers. Ideally these programs work in close cooperation with local school counselors, are under the direction of a professionally trained person, and involve volunteer workers who can work with youngsters over a long period even though the rate of progress might be quite limited.

4. *Interparish Projects.* In an effort to utilize their strength on behalf of more than their own parish, some churches have consciously sought opportunities for working closely with other churches, either with those in their immediate community or with others of more limited resources — perhaps in the inner city. In some cases a suburban congregation and a church in a transitional community joined forces to work on a specific project, perhaps sponsoring a vacation Bible school in the transition community. The suburban church provided the booklets and material needed and assisted by providing additional

teachers. All then worked together on the project itself. In another case an inner-city church desired to accept more neighborhood children into its school whose families were unable to pay the tuition. Because of limited finances they felt they could not enroll them free. A church with greater financial resources provided a dozen scholarships. One congregation in a prosperous Detroit suburb gave its building fund of $50,000 to assist an inner-city congregation. The money was used to help underwrite a halfway house for youth and a camp program for teen-agers.

In still other cases churches within the same area have joined efforts. In one city two churches, one white and the other Negro, joined their commissions on Christian social concern to concentrate on an economically depressed area close to both churches. After conversations were held for several months, a group of 20 men began to make personal calls on families moving into urban redevelopment housing projects. Their purpose was to indicate their desire to be of help to these families and to offer the services of their congregations.

A program of greater depth developed in a large Midwestern city. The work arose out of the contact between suburban and inner-city people. The goal was to establish an "outpost" to serve as a point of contact for both communities. It quickly became a center of information concerning such problems as employment, education, welfare, and urban renewal; it became a center for political action and volunteer community programs; it provided contact with hospitals and housing clinics, sources of aid for alcoholics and juvenile delinquents. The group hoped to establish a retreat house on the edge of the inner-city area where representatives from both communities might come for spiritual refreshment and training for Christian service in the metropolis.

5. Bridges to the Community. As churches have lifted their eyes to the world, they have become aware of need among people who may consciously or unconsciously reject help from the church. In compassion the church has desired to offer aid without running roughshod over the sensibilities of such people.

75

One group is composed of those young single persons who may feel alienated from family, church, and society. Often they seem alienated from themselves. The coffeehouse has provided a neutral setting in which the church has sought to meet this maverick group. Usually located in a basement-type setting near a heavy concentration of rooming houses for young singles, it sponsors a program of music, poetry readings, and discussion groups. Much of the entertainment is spontaneous; there is a great deal of free time during which the guests can talk among themselves or with those from the church who are serving on that particular evening.

A similar goal of opening avenues of discussion with those whom the church would not ordinarily meet has been reached through the establishment of bookstores. In contrast to the book service established primarily for those who are members, churches have opened this type of store away from the church premises and operate it as a means of establishing dialog with thoughtful people who may have dismissed the established church.

Churches also have addressed themselves to a specific sector of community life, such as the arts. Some have sponsored art festivals to demonstrate the church's concern for art and the artist. These festivals usually are held over a weekend. They might open with an evening of drama. The following day there are workshop sessions on the various arts. The gymnasium or other large facility is used as a gallery for the display of art. The weekend comes to a climax on Sunday with a major dramatic or musical offering. It has been suggested that the same technique could be used with other sectors of life, such as science, work, government and political structures, or education.

6. *Establishing Contact with the Economic and Political Structures of Society.* The work of the Detroit Industrial Mission is perhaps the finest example of a group wrestling with the question of how the church might minister more effectively to the structures of our industrial society. With few exceptions, this remains a field in which the church has been quite ineffec-

tive. Individual Christians may sense a tension between the criteria of efficiency and profit and the values of the Christian faith. The faith has been interpreted to most men as having only personal relevance; thus they have great difficulty in applying the insights of the faith to the tasks of decision-making or of evaluating corporate policy and structure. Most parish pastors are of minimal assistance because of their ignorance of the world of business and industry. Therefore from the pulpit they continue to give oversimplified moralistic answers to problems with which their men (and women) are wrestling.

As a step in the right direction individual Christians in a number of businesses have taken the initiative in calling together luncheon discussion groups. The quality of these meetings varies a great deal, as do their purposes. Some have deliberately broadened the group to include those who hold jobs on varying levels of responsibility. Others tend to concentrate on a specific level of worker or manager. Panels of men who have researched a given topic act as the resource for a given meeting. Others have attempted to bring in speakers who would help them grow in their understanding of the faith or in their understanding of the problem that may be before them.

Another mission field open to the church involves its responsibility to the local and broader community of which it is a part. Within recent years clergymen have expressed increased interest in understanding the nature of community, its power structures, its racial and ethnic groupings, its financial resources, and in general the broad range of problems and resources facing a given community.

Urban planning, for example, will assume an increasingly significant role in our society during this decade. One of the ranking city planners in the United States is a Christian layman of strong commitment and vision. He has invited the church to enter the dialog with others who are planning the metropolis of the future. With the aid of computers whole systems of the city can be simulated to indicate what a particular part of the population will look like in the future, what its educational or traffic needs will be 15 years from now. These men are serious about designing a city that will permit the fullest development of human life that our world has ever seen. This planner wants the church to be involved for the benefit that will accrue to the church as it becomes familiar with the discipline of planning and also for the benefit city planners will get from hearing the kinds of questions that the church is responsible for asking.

Church bodies that see the necessity for effecting change in the community are attempting to develop models for achieving transformation in a metropolitan community. They want to discover the role of the church in the decision-making echelons of the city. In one large city, for example, the church discovered that no public-housing units had been constructed in 12 years. Despite a growing need for such housing, the conservative concerns of those opposed to such governmental programs had prevented any movement. The decision has been made to identify the persons and groups capable of initiating public-housing projects and to investigate resources within the church for bringing about a favorable decision by the community organizations that should be involved. If a year of such effort appears to make no realistic progress, the plan is to begin the process of obtaining 100-percent government financing for a church-sponsored public-housing project. The churches would attempt to explain to the whole community why the church has taken this action. A team ministry will then be ready to serve the project without a church building as base of operations, in other words, with no "edifice complex."

A growing number of churches have had to face decisions regarding their potential participation in various types of community organizations.[2] Most of the difficulty has centered in the decision of whether to support programs that might generate hostility and conflict within the community. In one area, for example, there was a crying need to develop a basic sense of community in a diversified area of Poles, Italians, Negroes, Puerto Ricans, and Southern whites. The area needed new housing and the conservation of some of its old buildings. The churches saw a point for their own service. Monthly meetings were begun between the leaders of the Protestant and Roman

78

Catholic churches. Through their efforts a community conservation commission was established. As a result the community is a safer and cleaner place to live. Young people have been drawn together in constructive activity in place of their former destructive behavior. Sanitation has improved; housing codes are being enforced. The people have begun to respond to one another as members of a single community.

7. *Faith in Life Church-Community Dialogs.*[2] These dialogs are an American adaptation of the German *Kirchenwochen*. Their goal is to encourage the church to leave the sanctuary and move out into the world. Taking the structures of society seriously, they use churchmen with credentials so impeccable in a given profession that they can be accepted in their own right. Speakers take part in the regular gatherings of the community. Service clubs, movie houses, waiting rooms in hospitals, farmers' gathering places, the city hall, cafes and restaurants become places where members of the team, laymen and clergy alike, go to talk. By design their task is to begin dialog — not just to talk and analyze but to listen. Special gatherings are held with doctors, youth, the aged, parents, public officials, and pastors. In the larger communities radio and television are used heavily. In a 5-day period as much as 60 hours of radio and television — much of it prime time — may be used.

The programs have been stimulated by Lutherans, but they have been ecumenical in character. It was a significant experience for each churchman to enter this common mission to a given community, even while he knew that official unity among the denominations would be long in coming.

For several years a young clergyman has ministered on the Las Vegas Strip. The chaplain spends his time until about 4:00 a. m. each morning backstage at various shows, in cocktail lounges, casinos, coffee shops, and bars, contacting people in need. He conducts individual and group counseling sessions in the afternoons and early evenings. He would characterize his work primarily as a "listening ministry." He attempts to understand the people and the groups behind the glitter of Las Vegas. Many of the people he contacts are those who have been estranged from any relationship with the organized church because of their occupation, guilt, working hours, or group mores. His question is: What is God doing here, and to what service is He calling His people in this place? Plans are under way for the establishment of a coffeehouse of the type described earlier. Because this ministry is being carried out in a community that knows a high concentration of gambling, divorce, remarriage, drinking, suicides, show business, and high crime rates, the work done in Las Vegas should speak meaningfully to other communities.

8. New Forms Need Pastors. The new forms need pastors who are sensitive to our culture and have learned to reflect theologically about it. Too often traditional seminary training has failed to develop these outlooks and skills. Thus the questions of continuing education for the clergy and of specialized training have been raised. The Urban Training Center in Chicago is one of the most exciting educational experiments devised for meeting the latter need. Its goal is to train clergymen and laity in understanding the modern metropolis and their roles within it. Each year the center focuses on a major problem area to which it addresses itself. In its first year it focused on unemployment. The student learns by becoming involved. As the team members investigate different aspects of a problem, they attempt to understand it in its broader dimensions and to suggest appropriate ways by which the church might transform the situation. To this growing awareness they bring a set of theological questions: What is God doing here? How is the church called to gather around God's action in this event? How do we understand this particular group or movement as a manifestation of God's grace? In what ways are fields of action a means of God's love as well as instruments of sin? How does one incarnate himself into a neighborhood? How does one awaken people to the various crises in which they live?

9. A Nonstipendiary Ministry. The vast areas of need opening before the church today, coupled with the sobering fact that each decade records a decreased proportion of the world's population within the Christian church, demands that we consider ways of developing a nonstipendiary ministry of men in various specialized situations. We need these men in areas where good stewardship questions the advisability of sending an ordained graduate with some 10 years of specialized training: areas of the inner city thickly populated with lower-income people, rural areas of declining population, among groups of special language or culture such as communities of American Indians, special professional and occupational groups such as scientists, scholars, technologists, or artists. The goal of sending a few paid missionaries to groups such as these involves immense amounts of money and usually meets with only a modicum of success. Therefore a number of churches — outstanding among them the Episcopalian Church — are seriously investigating the possibility of establishing or expanding a nonstipendiary, self-supporting, ordained ministry. The goal would be to choose secularly employed persons who would remain in their chosen professions but as fully ordained clergymen would supplement the traditional pastoral and nonparochial ministries and chaplaincies. The Episcopalian study document said in part:

> Because the ministry of Word and Sacrament is central to the life and witness of our Church, new approaches to the selection, training, and deployment of deacons and priests are of the utmost importance. These new approaches can only be implemented if the Church is willing to move freely beyond the established pattern of existing stipendiary position.[3]

The experience of the Southwark group in London is instructive. At the present time some 50 percent of those entering the ordained ministry of the Church of England come from the working class. Contrary to expectation, however, these men have not been willing to move back into the urban parishes of South London. The average length of time that a man spends as rector or vicar of a parish in the inner city has been 2½ years. The report comes that these men no longer are able to mix freely with the people in the "back street" parishes; thus the unhappy pastors take the first opportunity to leave. A new ordination training center has been established which trains men for such ministries in a night-school course of theology that prepares them for ordination, but they will return to their full-time employment after ordination.[4]

The Major Affirmations and Questions That Emerge from This Overview of New Forms

a. The question of forms and structures is not the exclusive nor perhaps even the primary question that must be asked in our day. Some of our problems are not ecclesiological. We must examine forms, old and new, to make certain they are an expression of our convictions regarding the church.

b. In the current renewal we must deal with the center of church life and its underlying assumptions and not be content with achieving peripheral success. Important is the question of how we move experimental forms of ministry into the regular, ongoing life of the church.

c. In place of seeing the church as an institution occupying separate ground in our modern world, the new forms attempt to take the structures of society seriously and to enter them with the judgment and grace of God.

d. Instead of gaining advantage for the organized church, the new forms attempt to incarnate the servant role. The new forms work with a minimum of external structure. They acknowledge the expendable quality of their own existence.

e. The new forms work heavily with the concept of the church as the whole people of God. They attempt to use Christians in the richness of their relationships and in the fullness of the gifts which the Holy Spirit has given to them.

f. The new forms have demonstrated the need for greater flexibility in the selection, training, and development of men in ordained ministries. The immediate future will need an increasing number of men who will minister to segments of our society chosen on a basis other than that of residence.

g. Because of the scope and complexity of the challenges to which we are called, it is imperative that we define areas in which we will be able to address ourselves to broader concerns of the community on an ecumenical basis.

82

The church today is concerned that the Gospel live in the world. For it has rediscovered that God loves the world, not only the church. The church has rediscovered God's concern for the secular, not only the sacred. It realizes anew that God reconciled the entire world to Himself. Therefore the church exists *in the world* as that community which testifies to the presence of God in our age. In faithfulness to this task the church struggles for forms by which it can raise this witness. It does so with hope in the resurrected and reigning Lord.

NOTES FOR CHAPTER 5

[1] At one time it was necessary for the church to provide direct welfare service for those who lacked food, shelter, employment, and education. Now, because of the greater response of the public, the role of the church has shifted. Discussing this issue in 1965 the Board of National Missions of the United Presbyterian Church in the U. S. A. provided a useful analysis:

> Although the church will continue to be called to provide direct service in areas where alienation and suffering are critical and ignored, the *major* role of the church in serving persons in greated need will no longer be in the offering of direct church-administered social services. The church must assume a more active role in influencing public and private secular welfare policy and program. It must be concerned with fundamental policies in such areas as housing, education, and employment at the roots of poverty. It must participate in programs sponsored by secular agents.
>
> This more complex mission function will require the church to assume these roles:
>
> 1. To encourage public and private agencies and groups to serve the common good and to affirm and uphold them when they do.
> 2. To articulate an understanding of the nature and purpose of human life in community and to participate in defining values and goals for the whole community.
> 3. To act as a critic of public policy, assuming a function of constructive criticism in relation to any apparent shortcomings or perversions of any programs intended to help the poor.
> 4. To re-examine the program of the church itself, and the extent to which it assists or hinders assumption of responsibility by the whole community.
> 5. To seek ways in which the resources of the church in buildings, money, personnel, and dedicated membership may be most fully utilized in cooperation with and as part of community-wide programs of attack on poverty.

6. To give special attention to interdenominational and interfaith responsibility concerning poverty.
7. To encourage programs in which more affluent congregations and their members participate in action with Christians who live in areas of critical need.
8. Most of all, to give careful attention to the voice of the poor themselves in everything that has to do with them. A major form of direct service to the needy which the church can now perform is to provide such assistance as is required in order that their voices may influence the decisions being made about their own welfare.

[2] Cf. *Dialogue: Bridging Our Separate Worlds.* Published by the Faith in Life Dialogue, Northern Lakes Area (October 1965).

[3] *A Self-Supporting Ministry and the Mission of the Church.* By a group of sixty bishops, other clergy, and lay people of the Episcopal Church. Published by the Division of Christian Ministries of the National Council of the Episcopal Church. Cf. pp. 1 – 12.

[4] "Priests Who Don't Get Paid for It," *Church in Metropolis* (Quarterly publication of the National Council of the Protestant Episcopal Church), No. 2 (Summer 1964), pp. 27 – 30.

Date Due

47470